HEALING THE EMPTY NESTER'S GRIEVING HEART

D1414395

Also by Dr. Alan Wolfelt

Grief One Day at a Time:
365 Meditations to Help You Heal After Loss

Healing the Adult Child's Grieving Heart:
100 Practical Ideas After Your Parent Dies

Healing the Adult Sibling's Grieving Heart:
100 Practical Ideas After Your Brother or Sister Dies

Healing Your Grief About Aging:
100 Practical Ideas on Growing Older with
Confidence, Meaning, and Grace

The Mourner's Book of Hope:
30 Days of Inspiration

Understanding Your Grief:
Ten Essential Touchstones for Finding Hope and Healing Your Heart

When Your Pet Dies:
A Guide to Mourning, Remembering, and Healing

The Wilderness of Grief:
Finding Your Way

*Companion Press is dedicated to the education
and support of both the bereaved and bereavement
caregivers. We believe that those who companion
the bereaved by walking with them as they journey
in grief have a wondrous opportunity: to help others
embrace and grow through grief—and to lead
fuller, more deeply-lived lives themselves
because of this important ministry.*

Companion
PRESS

For a complete catalog and ordering information, write or call:

Companion Press
The Center for Loss and Life Transition
3735 Broken Bow Road
Fort Collins, CO 80526
(970) 226-6050
www.centerforloss.com

HEALING THE EMPTY NESTER'S GRIEVING HEART

•

100 PRACTICAL IDEAS FOR PARENTS AFTER THE KIDS MOVE OUT, GO OFF TO COLLEGE, OR START TAKING FLIGHT

•

ALAN D. WOLFELT, PH.D.

Companion
PRESS

Fort Collins, Colorado

An imprint of the Center for Loss and Life Transition

Companion Press is an imprint of the
Center for Loss and Life Transition
3735 Broken Bow Road
Fort Collins, Colorado 80526
www.centerforloss.com

26 25 24 23 22 21 20 19 18 17   5 4 3 2 1

ISBN: 978-1-617222-50-4

For my precious children—Megan, Chris, and Jaimie.

Thank you for allowing me the honor of being your parent.
I hope you know your mom and I will never stop adoring you.
Now, go out there into the world and enjoy the journey.

Love, Dad

CONTENTS

Introduction 1

1. Make plans for the big day 7
2. Practice owning—and communicating—your grief 8
3. Allow for numbness 9
4. Understand that your child is also grieving 10
5. Practice breathing in and out 11
6. Understand the six needs of mourning
   Need 1. Acknowledge that children leaving home is a
   significant life transition and loss 12
7. Understand the six needs of mourning
   Need 2. Learn to embrace the pain 13
8. Understand the six needs of mourning
   Need 3. Remember your life together with your child so far 14
9. Understand the six needs of mourning
   Need 4. Work on your changing self-identity 15
10. Understand the six needs of mourning
    Need 5. Find new ways to connect with your child 16
11. Understand the six needs of mourning
    Need 6: Accept help from others 17
12. Respect and communicate with your partner 18
13. Don't forget your other children 19
14. Start an empty-nest journal 20
15. Do nothing 21
16. If you're divorced, know that empty-nester grief
    can be more complicated 22
17. If you're a single parent, seek extra support 23
18. If you've been a stay-at-home parent, be extra-
    compassionate with yourself 24
19. If your child is an only, know that empty-nester grief
    can be more complicated 25
20. If you're a mother going through hormonal changes,
    work with your healthcare provider 26
21. Inventory your losses 27
22. Develop ways to wrangle the worry 28
23. Put together a small photo album or photo book for your child 29
24. Harness the power of intention 30
25. Cocoon 31
26. Embrace fear 32
27. Relearn how to take care of yourself 33

28. Make a plan for the first special days without your child   34
29. Ignore hurtful advice   35
30. Give your child some space   36
31. Declare your values   37
32. Notice five things   38
33. Practice spontaneity   39
34. Find ways to cope with the loneliness   40
35. Be on the watch for old griefs   41
36. Know that your body will grieve too   42
37. Give yourself time   43
38. Go off the deep end   44
39. Be aware of "borrowed tears"   45
40. Acknowledge your grief over your own aging   46
41. Seek help if you may be clinically depressed   47
42. Create new ways of connecting   48
43. Explore any regrets   49
44. Allow for resentment   50
45. Put plans on the calendar   51
46. Rebuild friendships   52
47. Recommit to (or rethink) your partner   53
48. Practice living in the now   54
49. Reacquaint yourself with you   55
50. Understand the difference between clean and dirty pain   56
51. Make time for spirituality   57
52. Leverage technology   58
53. Make friends with the empty bedroom   59
54. Believe in the power of "and"   60
55. Practice thinking, "I want…"   61
56. Renew intimacy   62
57. Consider your career   63
58. Build new communities   64
59. Reconsider the "empty" in "empty nest"   65
60. Think momentum   66
61. Ask yourself: What gives me joy?   67
62. Be grateful for your grief   68
63. Celebrate your heritage   69
64. Start new traditions   70
65. Spend your precious time on what really matters   71
66. Take lessons   72
67. Reconnect with your siblings   73

68. Dangle a carrot   74
69. Find the humor   75
70. Fix something   76
71. Work through dashed expectations or broken dreams   77
72. Expand your life to intersect with your independent child's   78
73. Empty the empty nest   79
74. Surround yourself with positivity   80
75. Review your finances   81
76. Spend more time with your own parents   82
77. Consider where you want to live   83
78. Say thank you   84
79. Get a kid fix   85
80. Enjoy what the earth has to offer   86
81. Work through estrangement   87
82. Let your hair down   88
83. Throw an empty-nest party   89
84. Beware of pressure-cooker syndrome   90
85. Take a digital reckoning   91
86. Act "as if"   92
87. See the world anew   93
88. Recapture your listening skills   94
89. Adopt a pet   95
90. Take a gap year   96
91. Savor the flavor of dining without kids   97
92. Date your partner   98
93. Move plans to the front burner   99
94. Grow yourself   100
95. Get ready to catch the boomerang   101
96. Imagine yourself at 96   102
97. Say the unsaid   103
98. Celebrate your parenting success   104
99. Know that parenting never ends   105
100. Place a photo where you'll see it often   106
A Final Word   107

INTRODUCTION

It can be so hard when our babies leave home. It's hard for us as parents, and it's often hard for our children, too—even if they're technically no longer children but instead young adults.

As our sons and daughters begin the process of moving out, heading off to college, or just generally asserting their independence, mothers and fathers often experience a mixture of difficult feelings. At one time or another, we might feel numbness, confusion, anxiety, sadness, hopelessness, anger, and/or regret. It's also common for us to feel some degree of relief and release as part of the mix.

But why are we having all these crazy, painful feelings? What are we supposed to *do* with them? And how can we move forward and re-infuse our own lives with renewed purpose and meaning?

I wrote this book to help all of us empty-nester parents explore and find answers to these questions. I have a particular interest in this topic because not only are my wife, Sue, and I parents to three young adults—Jaimie, Chris, and Megan, aged 21 to 28 at the time of this writing—I'm a grief counselor who travels the world educating people about the normal and necessary processes of grief and mourning. And even though I'm what others think of as an "expert" on grief and mourning, and despite the fact that I knew what to expect when I brought my first child to college 1,000 miles away, I still felt knocked flat by the force of my feelings of ambivalence and loss.

This book affirms that empty-nester grief is normal and necessary. It will help you not only weather the transition years but also strengthen your relationships with your partner and children, rediscover your own divine spark, and live fully and joyfully the rest of your days. Those are big promises. We'd better get started.

The empty nester

The phrase "empty-nest syndrome" was coined in the 1970s to describe the phase in our lives when our children begin leaving home. While people have been giving birth to children for millennia, of course, the modern-day practice of children routinely leaving home and moving away—often a great distance away—from their parents is a relatively new phenomenon. Not many decades ago, it was common for families to continue to live together, if not in the same house then at least in the same neighborhood or town. In fact, several generations often lived together under one roof.

What's more, life expectancies were somewhat shorter in past generations. I'm sure that my great-great-grandparents, too, experienced feelings of loss when their children took flight, but they and their peers could not always expect to live for three or four more decades beyond their active parenting years, as we are fortunate to.

Concurrent with the extension of life expectancies, parenting itself changed a great deal. The same advances that helped us live longer created opportunities for us to spend more and more resources on family and leisure activities. Just a few generations ago, most parents spent all their time working to provide their families with food and shelter. Today we devote ourselves to "parenting." We focus a great deal of our time, energy, money, and emotionality on our children. In doing so, we create more interdependent bonds than were common in past generations.

What's more, children used to become fully independent adults both at a younger age and more decisively. Today's twenty-somethings tend to hold onto their childhoods longer, creating a more extended and potentially more nebulous and challenging period of transition. Instead of fully claiming their independence, they often meander in and out of their parents' shelter and support for years. Just when you have them through college and think they're on their way, you find them perched back on the edge of your nest, looking out with trepidation or even laxity. "Fly!" you say. "It's rough out there," they say. "I think I'll go get a Starbucks."

I'm not saying that children and parents used to love each other less; I'm just pointing out that parent-child relationships were necessarily different in days gone by. The current-day form of the relationships we're fortunate to share with our offspring likely makes the transition to empty nesthood more difficult for both parties. I guess we're setting the stage for our children, who will probably draw on our modeling when it comes their turn to empty nest. That's a thought that inspires me to dig deep and model well.

The grief of transition

About 30 years ago I founded an organization called the Center for Loss and Life Transition. Even back then, fresh out of my Ph.D. program and a few years before my wife and I would have children, I understood that death is not the only loss that causes feelings of grief. All significant life transitions do.

You see, whenever we love someone or something, or whenever we feel a strong attachment to someone or something, we suffer feelings of grief when the attachment is disturbed. Death is the most extreme instance of this, of course, and most of us know firsthand about the grief caused by death. But all kinds of disturbances engender grief. For example, if we love a house that we have lived in for many years, we will experience pangs of grief when it comes time to move to a different house. If we divorce or retire from a longtime career, we grieve. Even when we move through ostensibly happy rites of passage, such as milestone birthdays or major wedding anniversaries, we not only celebrate, we also grieve what we are leaving behind.

For parents, our children's rites of passage affect us deeply. Raise your hand if you ever got teary-eyed when your kids blew out the candles on their birthday cakes, learned to ride a bike, went off to sleep-away camp for the first time, dressed up for prom, or tossed their graduation caps skyward. All those hands in the air—mine included—signal that many times already you've experienced the normal and necessary grief of parenting transitions.

Empty-nest grief is a grief of transition. It's the grief that accompanies significant change. It's also a grief of loss, however, because all transitions, even happy ones, harbor losses. Weddings are sappy—sad + happy—right?

Where does the sad come from? It comes from our grief over what's finished, what's lost. The bride and groom's childhoods. Their carefree youths. Their singlehood friends, activities, and lives. Their parents' bank accounts.

Speaking of which, right now Sue and I are involved in helping plan and pay for the wedding of our firstborn, Megan. We find ourselves experiencing these sappy feelings. In fact, it's a much more emotional process than we anticipated. As I imagine walking Megan down the aisle and "giving" her to her fiancé, Stephen, I experience a multitude of mixed emotions. My baby has grown up—and so have I. I'm getting old.

Likewise, our children's transitions to living on their own are also sappy. We celebrate their growth and burgeoning independence, of course—not to mention our own renewed freedom, but at the same time, we grieve over what's finished, what's lost. As we'll discuss in the pages to come, there are steps we can take to integrate this natural and necessary grief into our continued living. We can take action. Doing so will help us move forward.

How to use this book

As promised, this book contains 100 practical ideas to help heal your grieving heart. Some of the ideas will teach you about the principles of empty-nester grief and mourning. One of the most important ways to help yourself is to learn about the grief experience; the more you know, the less likely you will be to unknowingly perpetuate some of our society's harmful myths about grief and healing.

The remainder of the 100 ideas offer practical, here-and-now, action oriented tips for embracing your empty-nester grief. Each idea is followed by a brief explanation of how and why the idea might help you.

You'll also notice that each of the 100 ideas suggests a *carpe diem*, which means, as fans of the movie *Dead Poets Society* will remember, "seize the day." My hope is that you will not relegate this book to your shelves but keep it handy on your nightstand or desk. Pick it up often and turn to any page; the *carpe diem* suggestion will help you seize the day by helping you move toward healing today, right now, right this minute. If you come to an idea that doesn't seem to fit you, ignore it and flip to a different page.

It's my life's passion to help people grieve and mourn well so that they can go on to live and love well. You're at one of those critical junctures in your life when a little extra compassion, encouragement, and support can ensure you stay on the path that leads to healing and fulfillment. I'm gratified that this book can be your guide. Thank you for entrusting me to accompany you.

Alan D. Wolfelt

1.

MAKE PLANS FOR THE BIG DAY

"Making the decision to have a child is momentous. It is to decide forever to have your heart go walking around outside your body."
— Elizabeth Stone

- If you'll be taking your child to college or helping him move into his first apartment, you have an opportunity to prepare yourself beforehand for the emotions the day will bring.

- Think ritual. Most other similarly momentous life-transition days have a structure to help us get through them. Weddings, for example, usually include roles for the parents to play, such as walking the bride down the aisle, the mother-son or father-daughter dance, gift-giving, and toast-making.

- Consider creating small rituals for your child's moving day. For instance, you might write a letter to your child ahead of time and leave it on her pillow in her new room. The process of writing this letter will help you express your thoughts and feelings, and maybe shed a few tears. On moving day you'll be freer to focus on the chaos and physical demands of lugging boxes and last-minute shopping.

- Other ritual ideas for moving day: a celebration meal at a special restaurant; presenting your child with a wrapped, token or handmade gift; printing out a special poem and tacking it on his bulletin board; packing a care package ahead of time and hiding it in her closet for her to discover later (you can always text a clue!); framing a small print of a family photo and placing it on your child's dresser before you leave; and taking a series of snapshots or short video clips on moving day so you can make a social-media collage or video when you get home.

CARPE DIEM

If moving day's still ahead of you, make plans and add deadlines to your calendar so you'll be ready. If moving day's behind you, you can still frame a family photo and give it to your child as a "just-because" gift.

2.

PRACTICE OWNING—AND COMMUNICATING—YOUR GRIEF

"As a parent, it's my responsibility to equip my child to do this—to grieve when grief is necessary and to realize that life is still profoundly beautiful and worth living despite the fact that we inevitably lose one another."

— Sam Harris

- You wake up today, and you're just feeling sad. You enter your child's empty bedroom to retrieve something, and now you're even sadder. You're experiencing your grief. It's not fun, but it's true. Your grief is normal and necessary. It's your reality right now.

- Your coworker picks up on your mood and asks what's wrong. If you answer, "Oh nothing. I'm fine," you're not owning your grief. You're denying it. Instead, try, "I'm feeling blue because Jaimie's not home." Let the conversation unspool naturally from there.

- Ask your partner or a friend for a hug because you're feeling sad. Put your thoughts and emotions into words. Encourage your partner to express his or her thoughts and emotions too.

- If you have other kids at home, find moments to connect with them individually. Ask how they're doing. Let them know how you're doing. Be honest and loving.

CARPE DIEM
Say your grief out loud to someone today. Be honest and forthcoming about precisely what you're feeling.

3.

ALLOW FOR NUMBNESS

*"I've perfected the art of the fake smile. It's not so difficult
when you are completely numb."*

— Bethany Griffin

- Often, the first feeling we experience during or after a loss of any kind is numbness. We may feel shocked and in disbelief. This is nature's way of protecting us from the full force of a difficult reality all at once.

- Don't be surprised if you feel numb or even apathetic for a while. It doesn't mean you don't love or miss the child who's moved out; it just means it's such a new and surprising experience to your psyche that it might take some time for deeper feelings to bubble to the surface.

- Denial is a close relative of shock, numbness, and disbelief. Because we as a culture aren't very good at grief, we tend to encourage people to deny their true thoughts and feelings of loss. Are you having any twinges that you're suppressing? Are you finding yourself avoiding talking to others about your child's departure? Are you staying away from the empty bedroom so you don't have to think about it? These are all signs of denial, and while shock and numbness are normal and protective for a short period of time, ongoing denial will only result in long-term emotional problems such as anxiety and depression. You need to feel it to heal it.

CARPE DIEM
If you're feeling numb, cancel any optional commitments and
cozy up at home until you feel ready to emerge again.

4.

UNDERSTAND THAT YOUR CHILD IS ALSO GRIEVING

"Parents are the ultimate role models for children. Every word, movement, and action has an effect. No other person or outside force has a greater influence on a child than the parent."

— Bob Keeshan

• When it comes time to leave home, some children seem excited, and some seem scared. Some call, text, or visit home frequently; others, barely at all.

• No matter where your child's behavior falls on this continuum, however, she is almost certainly grieving inside to some extent. Even if she's thrilled about her new living arrangements, she is undoubtedly also experiencing pangs of loss. She might be missing old friends, her old school or workplace, her old room, pets, siblings, and yes, you.

• The six needs of mourning we'll soon review (Ideas 6 to 11) apply to your grieving child too. He also needs to learn to acknowledge and embrace painful feelings, integrate remembering into living, figure out his changing self-identity, find ways to stay connected with the meaningful parts of his "old life," and accept help from others. When you heap these tasks on top of all his other life demands, he has a lot on his plate.

• You can help your child learn to cope with all of life's challenges by openly expressing your own feelings and by accepting hers without judging or trying to fix them. It's normal for us as parents to want to solve our children's problems, but now that our children are young adults, we help best by being role models, mentors, and advisors— not fix-it-uppers.

CARPE DIEM
Be a mentor in grief. Let your child know you're
feeling blue about her leaving.

5.

PRACTICE BREATHING IN AND OUT

"Breath is the link between mind and body."
— Dan Brule

- Sometimes what we need most is just to "be." In our goal-oriented society, many of us have lost the knack for simply living.

- Drop all your plans and obligations for today and do nothing.

- Meditate if meditation helps center you. Find someplace quiet, be still, close your eyes and focus on breathing in and out. Relax your muscles. Listen to your own heartbeat.

- Breathing opens you up. Your grief may have closed you down. The power of breath helps to fill your empty spaces. The old wisdom of "count to ten" is all about taking a breath to open up space for something else to happen.

- Consciously breathe in and out; you can slow the world down and touch the edges of your true self.

CARPE DIEM

Right now, try this basic breathing exercise: Sit still, close your eyes, and begin to breathe through your nose. Inhale for a count of three, hold the breath for a count of one, exhale gently to a count of four, then hold the breath out for a count of one. Repeat five times.

6.

UNDERSTAND THE SIX NEEDS
OF MOURNING

Need 1. Acknowledge that children leaving home is a significant life transition and loss

"You don't really understand human nature unless you know why a child on a merry-go-round will wave at his parents every time around— and why his parents will always wave back."

— William D. Tammeus

- One of the main purposes of this book is to affirm that empty-nester grief is real and justified. For parents, children leaving home is a significant life transition. It leaves many losses in its wake.

- While empty-nest grief is not included in the Diagnostic and Statistical Manual—the guide that caregivers use to diagnose mental health problems—it's still a common, nameable challenge. And no, it's not a disorder! It's not "unhealthy"! It's simply normal, natural, and necessary grief.

- Yet empty-nest grief tends to be minimized in our culture. We sometimes shame mothers and fathers who struggle with their children leaving home. We imply that if they're grieving, they're overly and unhealthily attached. That is generally not true.

- If you are experiencing difficult thoughts and feelings over your child taking flight, you are grieving. You are normal. Your grief is necessary. You should not feel ashamed.

CARPE DIEM
Today, talk to someone you know to be compassionate about your normal, necessary empty-nester grief.

7.

UNDERSTAND THE SIX NEEDS OF MOURNING

Need 2. Learn to embrace the pain

"People are taught that pain is evil and dangerous. Pain is a feeling. Your feelings are part of you. Your own reality. If you feel ashamed of them, and hide them, you're letting society destroy your reality. You should stand up for your right to feel your pain."

— Jim Morrison

- One of your most important tasks in the weeks and months ahead is learning to befriend the pain you feel over your child gaining independence. You must lean into your pain instead of turning away from it.

- Sounds counterintuitive, right? That's because our culture misunderstands the role of pain and suffering. We mistakenly believe that everyone should try to feel all happy, all the time. We think emotional pain is bad, which is why, when Sue and I took Megan to her out-of-state college orientation her freshman year, the school psychologist advised us parents to "buck up" and "carry on." Bad advice.

- The truth is that emotional pain is often necessary. Like physical pain, emotional pain is there for a reason. It's trying to teach us something. We can't and shouldn't try to go around it. As Robert Frost famously wrote, "The best way out is always through."

- Always remember that your pain is part of your love for your child. How can you not cherish it?

- When you are feeling your empty-nester grief, allow yourself to feel it. Sit with it and let it move through you. Cry if you feel like crying. Tell someone what you're feeling. Feel it so that you can take a step toward healing it.

CARPE DIEM
Set aside 15 minutes today to sit with your pain. Be present to your thoughts and feelings, whatever they are.

8.

UNDERSTAND THE SIX NEEDS OF MOURNING

Need 3. Remember your life together with your child so far

"When you have brought up kids, there are memories you store directly in your tear ducts."
— Robert Brault

- There are times in our lives when we naturally pause to take stock of all that has come before. This is one of those times. We naturally look back before we look forward.

- To prepare for their children's high school graduations, parents often pull out snapshots from throughout their children's lives and arrange them in photo albums, memory boxes, poster displays, and videos. It's instinctual, this need to review the story and see all its parts and pieces in one place.

- Working on memory tasks will help you acknowledge your empty-nester grief and embrace the pain. Any completed albums, books, or videos will also help your child move from this chapter of his life to the next.

- Sit down with your child and look over photos and videos together if possible. Sharing your intermingled grief and joy in this manner will help tie a strong knot in your relationship and your joint stories so far—a knot that both of you will hold onto as you continue to climb.

CARPE DIEM
Spend some time with photos or videos of your child today. During or after, talk to someone about any thoughts and feelings that arise.

9.

UNDERSTAND THE SIX NEEDS OF MOURNING

Need 4. Work on your changing self-identity

"The one thing about being a parent is the ability to be selfless: to give up the things you want and need for the benefit of someone else."
— Danny McBride

- This is a major mourning need for empty-nester parents. When our children leave home, we lose many roles, responsibilities, and connections that shaped who we have been over the past two decades. These losses often throw us into disarray.

- Who are we now, if we're not first and foremost the parents of (fill in your child's name here)? What will take the place of all those responsibilities and connections we used to have? What do we want to do with the rest of our lives?

- It will probably take a long time for us to find answers to these questions. Along the way, we'll be mourning the loss of our old identities. There's no rush or timetable we have to meet. Let's keep in mind that the journey is what it's all about.

- I hope that in addition to the pain, you also feel the glimmers of hope and excitement that I do over the possibilities of the years to come. Our changing self-identities can accommodate all kinds of thoughts and feelings—sad, happy, scared, excited, everything.

CARPE DIEM
How are you feeling today about your self-identity? Share your thoughts and feelings with someone who cares about you.

10.

UNDERSTAND THE SIX NEEDS
OF MOURNING

Need 5. Find new ways to connect with your child

"Piglet sidled up to Pooh from behind. 'Pooh!' he whispered. 'Yes, Piglet?'
'Nothing,' said Piglet, taking Pooh's paw. 'I just wanted to be sure of you.'"
— A.A. Milne

- When our children leave home, we lose our daily connections with them.
  Even though they've been busy teenagers, with lives of their own, we still
  got to see them regularly. We might have had dinner, watched TV, or
  played with the dog together. We also shared special times, like meals out
  or shopping trips. Now that they're no longer under the same roof with
  us, we often feel disconnected from them, which rouses our grief.

- Learning to live with that new disconnection is part of our grief. It's a
  change and a loss. We must find ways to mourn it openly and fully. We
  must become reconciled to it.

- But finding new ways to connect with our young adult children is
  also part of our journey. How will we communicate with each other?
  How often? When will we see them? Consider the past meaning of
  your life with your child, and look to the future to build on top of that
  foundation of meaning.

- As with all major life transitions, this one will naturally take some time
  to sort itself out. There are no "right ways" to do it. All we as parents
  can offer is our unconditional love as our children work on establishing
  their independence. And as we find new, precious ways to connect, if
  only for a few short minutes or hours here and there, we can learn new
  ways to treat them as the lifelong treasures they are.

CARPE DIEM
Call, text, or write your child right now and let him
know you're thinking about him.

11.

UNDERSTAND THE SIX NEEDS OF MOURNING

Need 6. Accept help from others

"Until we can receive with an open heart, we're never really giving with an open heart. When we attach judgment to receiving help, we knowingly or unknowingly attach judgment to giving help."
— Brené Brown

- Parents are usually the helpers, right? If you need something done, ask a mom or a dad, the saying goes. We're good at multitasking, organizing, doing, and helping others.

- But now…now we're the ones who need the help. That can be a hard thing to admit and accept. After all, we just spent the last 20-odd years being super humans.

- Surrendering to our normal and necessary grief means acknowledging that we have been laid low by it. We're not invincible after all. We're tender, and we're hurting.

- Accepting help from others during our time of empty-nester grief means allowing them to take care of us. We will gratefully accept their companionship. We will talk and let them listen. We will also let them take on the responsibilities of multitasking, organizing, and doing for the time being. Right now, we need to take off our capes and rest for a while.

CARPE DIEM
Reach out to someone today and let them know you need their help and companionship.

12.

RESPECT AND COMMUNICATE WITH YOUR PARTNER

*"To be fully seen by somebody, then, and be loved anyhow—
this is a human offering that can border on miraculous."*
— Elizabeth Gilbert

- Even in the same household, parents parent differently. You'll find that you and your partner will navigate the waters of empty-nester grief differently too. My wife, Sue, and I are a reflection of the "complementary theory of relationship." In other words, opposites attract. We are very different and have naturally experienced very different thoughts and feelings about the transition to empty nesting after raising three children together.

- You and your partner will not share all the same thoughts and feelings over your child's departure. That's normal. Grief is unique to each person and each loss.

- Be respectful of your partner's thoughts and feelings, even if they're vastly different than your own. Try to learn more about and empathize with his or her point of view.

- Talk often with your partner about everything—including the empty-nest experience. Not only is communication key to relationship satisfaction, it's essential to supporting one another in your grief.

- What to do if you're not respecting or communicating well? See a counselor. If you intend to stay together after the children are gone, now's the time to work on your marriage or partnership. Your current well-being and future happiness depend on it.

CARPE DIEM
Sit face-to-face with your partner today, turn off all distractions, hold hands, and have a quiet, loving conversation about your child's departure.

13.

DON'T FORGET YOUR OTHER CHILDREN

"Sibling relationships outlast marriage, survive the death of parents, resurface after quarrels that would sink any friendship. They flourish in a thousand incarnations of closeness and distance, warmth, loyalty, and distrust."

— Erica E. Goode

- When one child moves out, the siblings are affected too, especially if they still live at home.

- Don't underestimate their grief, even if they seem like they're doing fine. I often call grieving siblings "forgotten mourners," because it can be easy to overlook them, especially when we're so distracted by our own grief and other life demands. Our youngest, Jaimie, idolized (and still does) her big brother, Chris. She needed support and understanding when he went off to college.

- Teenagers and young adults tend to hide their feelings from parents and other in-charge grown-ups. They're in that developmental phase when their job is to separate from their parents, so they're usually more connected to their friends and peers at this time. Yet they usually won't talk to their friends about any struggles they might be having over their sibling's departure.

- Find ways to spend one-on-one time with your children who are still living at home. They're more likely to open up to you if you're doing an activity together, such as shooting baskets or shopping, than if you approach them directly just to talk. Think sideways, not head-on.

- Keep in mind that the whole family dynamic is changing, so not only might remaining children miss the child who moved away, they might also be having a hard time with increased parental attention on them or perceived pressure to follow in their sibling's footsteps. Treat them with extra care, kindness, and patience.

CARPE DIEM
Spend some one-on-one time today with any children who are still at home. Commit to yourself to touch base with them in a focused, present way at least once a day from now on.

14.

START AN EMPTY-NESTER JOURNAL

"Writing is an intense form of self-exploration, and through thoughtful encounters with the humble self, we grow, and that growth diminishes unhappiness and creates joy."

— Kilroy J. Oldster

- If you've never tried journaling before, now might be a good time to give it a go.

- Get a blank notebook and a pen you like writing with—or you can use a laptop. I suggest spending five minutes writing first thing every morning or last thing before bed every night.

- The purpose of the journal is to express your thoughts and feelings about your child moving out. Writing is a form of mourning, and it will help you heal.

- If you need a little structure for your daily writing, consider writing about your grief for two minutes and your gratitude for two minutes. Anything having to do with your child's departure goes under grief—whether it's happy, sad, or in between—and notes about anything you felt grateful for that day—big or little—goes under gratitude.

- Over the course of months, you'll be able to look back on your earlier journal entries and see your progress and growth.

CARPE DIEM

Start your journal today. It can be on paper or on your computer or phone. Pick a time to write in it for a few minutes each day. Set a reminder on your phone.

15.

DO NOTHING

"The one thing children wear out faster than shoes is parents."
— John J. Plomp

- When their last child takes flight, most of the parents I know have shared with me the same sentiment: "Whew! We made it!"

- Make no mistake, parenting is exhausting labor. Like my friends, what you might find yourself in need of most right now is rest and relaxation.

- Besides, your natural and necessary grief might be calling on you to withdraw for a while. (See Idea 25.) If so, surrender to it. Go into neutral before you get into gear again.

- Wallow in inactivity. Be a sloth. You need and deserve it. When you're well-rested and your initial, acute grief has subsided some, you'll be ready for more active mourning and re-engaging with the world.

CARPE DIEM
Lie on your bed with your arms and legs outstretched and your eyes closed. Listen to your own heartbeat. Breathe deeply. Practice daily until you're comfortable doing nothing for at least 15 minutes.
Bonus points if you fall asleep.

16.

IF YOU'RE DIVORCED, KNOW THAT EMPTY-NESTER GRIEF CAN BE MORE COMPLICATED

"When two divorced people marry, four people get into bed."
— Jewish Proverb

- Split families can create complicated dynamics at empty-nesting time. Typically (but not always!), the more decision-making adults there are, the more complex the situation.

- Maybe your children are starting to take flight, and your new spouse doesn't share your grief. Or maybe your newly independent children are spending more of their precious free time with your ex than they are with you. Or now that child support is ending, maybe one parent is unfairly having to shoulder a disproportionate amount of a young adult's independent living or college costs. Stepparent and blended sibling situations can also muddy the waters.

- Non-judgmental, non-blaming communication is important right now. While you can't control how others will communicate or respond, you can control your communication. Strive to be open, loving, and honest. Let others know how you're feeling and why. Ask for what you want and need.

- Seek support outside the family as well. A good friend can be an objective sounding board and advocate.

CARPE DIEM
Schedule a parent meeting to talk about any empty-nest situations that have been troubling you. Include any stepparents, if appropriate.

17.

IF YOU'RE A SINGLE PARENT, SEEK EXTRA SUPPORT

"We do everything but leap tall buildings in a single bound.
We are superheroes without capes."
— Debbie Burgin

- Understandably, single parents often have uniquely close relationships with their children. After all, as they grew you became a team, with all of you having to share the responsibilities of the household to some extent. This dynamic tends to make children of single parents more responsible, independent, and eventually peers to their parent instead of children.

- Empty-nester parents without partners often have such close relationships with their children that they feel lost when the children take flight. The children, too, can have a harder time with the transition because they feel guilty about leaving their parent alone. They are at risk for stalling developmentally. If you see this, be sure to let your children know they are not responsible for you and encourage them to launch into the next phase of their lives.

- If you're a single parent struggling with empty-nester grief, be sure to reach out for help. Other single parents can be a great source of affirmation and comfort. If other adults have been part of your support system, such as your own parents or family members or a close set of friends, turn to them now. Be open and honest about your pain and practical challenges. Let others help you. You need your network now as much as when your kids were little.

- If you don't have a good support network, professional counseling might be a great resource. After all, you need to talk out your thoughts and feelings with someone, and a compassionate counselor will know how to help you through the transition and on to your new life.

CARPE DIEM
Ask someone today for a bit of help. Tomorrow, ask someone else.

18.

IF YOU'VE BEEN A STAY-AT-HOME PARENT, BE EXTRA-COMPASSIONATE WITH YOURSELF

"When in doubt, choose the kids.
There will be plenty of time later to choose work."
— Anna Quindlen

- If you've devoted yourself fully to raising your children, it's only natural that your empty-nester grief will be particularly difficult. With grief, the rule of thumb is this: the stronger the attachment that has been disturbed, the stronger the resulting grief.

- The word "compassion" literally means "with passion." Practicing self-compassion means caring for yourself with passion. All that passion you poured into raising your children? It's time to pour it on yourself.

- Some stay-at-homers are chomping at the bit to re-engage with their own lives after their children leave home. If this is you, go for it! But if you're among the stay-at-home parents feeling profound empty-nester grief, I urge you to be patient with yourself and seek extra support. Arrange coffee dates with other empty nesters. Join an online group or forum. See a counselor. Strong grief requires strong support.

- Even as you're grieving and mourning, don't forget to celebrate your accomplishments as a stay-at-home parent. You devoted a great deal of your life to ensuring that your children were well cared for. Consider taking a special trip or arranging whatever reward you would most enjoy to thank yourself.

CARPE DIEM
I'll say it again: strong grief requires strong support.
Reach out for help today.

19.

IF YOUR CHILD IS AN ONLY, KNOW THAT EMPTY-NESTER GRIEF CAN BE MORE COMPLICATED

"Love the whole world as a mother loves her only child."
— Guatama Buddha

- For parents with at least two children, the empty-nest journey gets spread out over more kids and usually more years. It's dispersed and often relatively gradual. It's less like ripping off a Band-aid.

- If you're the parent of an only child—a child who is now taking flight—it's normal for your grief experience to be more challenging. You know how a four-legged animal can still walk and even run if it loses one leg? Your family is more like a three-legged stool, and now it is losing a leg. How can you possibly remain upright?

- So what can you do? Make every effort to talk openly and non-judgmentally with your partner or a friend about your grief. Acknowledge and embrace the complicated nature of your loss experience. Understanding and accepting that your grief may be particularly painful will help you, ironically, weather the pain.

- Find ways to mourn together with your partner, if possible. Reach out to friends and extended family members. And above all, be patient and gentle with yourself.

CARPE DIEM

If your child is an only and you're having a hard time getting through the day, look into scheduling an appointment with a counselor. A little extra conversation and support will help.

20.

IF YOU'RE A MOTHER GOING THROUGH HORMONAL CHANGES, WORK WITH YOUR HEALTHCARE PROVIDER

"I'm what is known as perimenopausal. 'Peri,' some of you may know, is a Latin prefix meaning 'Shut your flippin' pie hole.'"
— Celia Rivenbark

• Empty-nester timing is such that mothers often have to deal with the one-two punch of menopause and children leaving home at the same time (and possibly, in addition, elderly parents).

• Fluctuating or diminishing hormones can compound emotional stress and feelings of depression or anxiety. Insomnia makes everything worse. Menopause is hard enough. Menopause on top of other life changes can be overwhelming.

• See your healthcare provider for a routine exam. During your conversation, don't downplay any symptoms you may be having, physical or emotional.

• Your provider may suggest medical or complementary therapies that can help lessen or soothe your worst symptoms, which will also help soften your grief.

CARPE DIEM
Talk to several menopausal friends to see what's working for them.

21.

INVENTORY YOUR LOSSES

"All great changes are preceded by chaos."
— Deepak Chopra

- The major life transition of a child leaving home creates many losses in its wake. It's these losses that give rise to your thoughts and feelings of grief. Taking an inventory of all the losses can help you begin to understand and embrace your feelings about them.

- The first and most obvious loss is the missing presence of your child in your home. She's not there anymore! She's gone. Her absence creates a hole wherever she used to be.

- What other losses has your child's newfound independence created? When my daughter Megan left for university, I mourned how our family felt so different without her around, and my wife lost a confidant. Yes, the whole is greater than the sum of its parts.

- You might also be feeling a loss of security, for instance. When all your children were under your roof, you knew they were safe. Now you can no longer watch over them. I call this a "ripple-effect loss."

- Other ripple-effect losses for empty nesters may include a loss of identity, self-confidence, financial security (if you're funding your child's college or other expenses), health (if you're experiencing physical symptoms of grief or psychic symptoms, such as anxiety or depression), and hopes and dreams (if you saw your child's future going one way but it's actually going another).

CARPE DIEM
Make a written inventory of all the losses, big and small,
created by your child's departure.

22.

DEVELOP WAYS TO WRANGLE THE WORRY

"Your love, not your worry, is the most valuable thing any of us can give our children."
— Jason E. Royle

- We worry about our kids. That's what parents do. The leaving-home years are often when we worry most of all. In my experience, this adage is true: Little kids, little problems. Big kids, big problems. That's because adult missteps can have serious, long-lasting, and expensive consequences.

- So of course we worry, but at the same time, we know that worrying doesn't help. Worrying is anticipating a problem that's likely to not even happen. All it does is flood our bodies with stress hormones, causing us to lose sleep, gain weight, up our risk for cardiovascular disease, and sprout even more gray hairs.

- If your worry is affecting your health, it's time to see your physician and/or a counselor. They can work with you on tools to lower your anxiety, such as biofeedback, talk therapy, cognitive-behavioral therapy, medication, and more.

- On your own, you can try avoiding alcohol, reducing your caffeine intake, committing to regular exercise, getting more sunlight, quitting smoking, eating better, and meditating.

- You won't be able to thrive in and enjoy your empty-nest years if you're consumed by worry. Plus, it can kill you. Getting it under control should be your top priority.

CARPE DIEM
The next time you find yourself worrying about your child, ask yourself: how can I turn this worry into active, positive love?

23.

PUT TOGETHER A SMALL PHOTO ALBUM OR PHOTO BOOK FOR YOUR CHILD

"What I like about photographs is that they capture a moment that's gone forever, impossible to reproduce."
— Karl Lagerfeld

- Your child can take her family with her when she goes if she has a photo album or book to flip through whenever she's missing you.

- Of course, the process of putting the album together is healing for you too. The third need of mourning (Idea 8) is to remember your life together with your child so far.

- I'd suggest a small album or book, something your child can easily fit in his bedside drawer or on a bookshelf. The point isn't to include every photo that's ever been taken of him and his family but instead to curate a selection of the most special photos, one for each of the most important people and places in his life.

- This album or book would make a good gift to leave behind in your child's apartment or dorm room on moving day, or would be equally special mailed in a care package, together with a few treats, a few months later.

CARPE DIEM
Start working on a photo album or book for your child.

24.

HARNESS THE POWER OF INTENTION

"Every journey begins with the first step of articulating the intention, and then becoming the intention."
— Bryant McGill

- Do you ever feel like your life is a raging river and you're a twig being carried along by the strong, indiscriminate current? Do you feel anxious about your lack of control?

- It's true that in many ways, we as human beings have little control over our own lives. Things happen to us and to those we love that we would never choose.

- Yet even in the midst of the raging river, we can determine how we will respond to what happens to us. We can set our intention to live courageously and on purpose.

- I'm a big believer in actively and clearly setting your intention all along life's path. For us empty nesters, that might mean envisioning a future in which we are fulfilled, positive, whole individuals as well as engaged partners, parents, and grandparents. Even as we experience and live through our grief, at the same time we also set our intention to transcend our grief and attain even higher levels of fulfillment and joy.

CARPE DIEM

Fill in the blanks: Over time, I intend to fill my empty-nester years with _____, _____, and _____. I will be _____ and _____.

25.

COCOON

"What is a cozy home? Where you enter and you feel the radiance of your divine self."
— Harbhajan Singh Yogi

- Especially in the early weeks and months of your empty-nester grief, you may feel compelled to hole up in your house and withdraw from the world. This is a normal part of early grief.

- I often say that you must descend before you can transcend. In other words, the impulse to turn inward and slow down is a good one. It helps you sit with and experience your normal, necessary pain. It gives you the time and peace you need to understand what you are feeling and consider what to do about it.

- Think of yourself in emotional intensive care. This significant life transition has hit you hard. As after a serious physical injury, you may need some rest and recovery time before you can get moving again.

- If you feel like cocooning, cocoon! Drop any unnecessary commitments. Stock up on comfort food. Get into your jammies. Rest. Read. Watch TV. Cry if you feel like crying. Allow yourself to wallow.

- Don't feel guilty about cocooning, even if it's not something you would normally do. It's a temporary respite, and it's helping you recuperate.

CARPE DIEM
Plan some cocooning time into your day.

26.

EMBRACE FEAR

"Too many of us are not living our dreams because we are living our fears."
— Les Brown

- Part of our empty-nester grief is fear. We're afraid of what the transition will bring. Will we be OK? Will our children be OK? What if we're never as happy again as we were when our precious family members were all under one roof?

- While our fears are natural, they're also tamable. The trick lies in befriending them. First we must acknowledge our fears. Saying them aloud helps. Talking to others about them makes them less powerful. Journaling them also diminishes them.

- Then, holding our fears by the hand, we must step forward anyway. After all, we don't really have a choice. And what's the worst that could happen?

- Practice embracing fear by doing one thing every day that scares you at least a little. Each day, think of something you want to do but haven't tried. It's likely that between you and that want lies a patch of fear. You're afraid to try it, or you don't know how it works. Take a small step into the fear patch. Make a phone call, set up an appointment, check a book out from the library, reach out and ask a question.

- When you get better at stepping out of your comfort zone—and seeing that your imagined fears weren't so scary after all, you'll be ready to tackle bigger fears. Mending broken relationships. Traveling. Skydiving! Once you learn to embrace fear, there'll be no stopping you.

CARPE DIEM
Do something today that you've been wanting to do but that scares you.

27.

RELEARN HOW TO TAKE CARE OF YOURSELF

"Nourishing yourself in a way that helps you blossom in the direction you want to go is attainable, and you are worth the effort."

— Deborah Day

- As parents, we get really good at taking care of other people, but we often forget how to take care of ourselves.

- Yet you need and deserve good self-care, especially now, during this difficult time of transition. It's time to take all those great caregiver skills you've developed as a parent and apply them to yourself.

- Feed yourself well. Dress yourself well. Groom yourself well. Entertain yourself well. Get excellent medical care for yourself. Make sure you get enough sleep and physical activity. Give yourself fun money. Be kind to yourself. Be gentle and self-forgiving.

- If you're having a hard time practicing good self-care, consider this: Your adult children still need you, your partner and/or friends still need you, and the grandchildren you may one day have will need you too. You're at the age where attentive self-care may mean the difference between a premature departure and sticking around for a long time to come.

CARPE DIEM
Parent yourself well today. What will you do differently or better?

28.

MAKE A PLAN FOR THE FIRST SPECIAL DAYS WITHOUT YOUR CHILD

"Your body is away from me, but there is a window open from my heart to yours."
— Jalaluddin Rumi

- Birthdays, anniversaries, holidays, and other special family days can be really hard when our children aren't home to celebrate with us.

- Look at the next few months on the calendar and note which special days your child might not be present for. Now think about whether you want to reconfigure your usual celebration in any way. Planning ahead will help you feel a little more in control and prepared.

- You might choose to go ahead with the celebration as usual but add in a Skype call to your child in the middle of it. Or you might decide to send your child a care package ahead of time so he can celebrate there while you're celebrating here. Or maybe you want to eliminate some aspects of your usual tradition while adding in others. For example, you could skip the big family-cooked meal and go out for brunch instead, or you could invite friends or neighbors over to round out your festivities.

- Don't forget to ask your child if she has any thoughts about the celebration. After all, she's still an important part of your family, even if she's no longer living at home. And being open about feelings helps everyone. Besides, she just might have creative ideas you haven't thought of, or she might have great plans of her own, which might put your mind and heart at ease.

CARPE DIEM
With your partner or a close friend, brainstorm possibilities for the next special day without your child.

29.

IGNORE HURTFUL ADVICE

"Nobody can give you wiser advice than yourself."
— Cicero

• As a culture, we're generally not very good at being present to others in pain. In fact, we often try to shame them or deny their pain. Grieving empty nesters are sometimes told, "You knew this day was coming," "You were fortunate to have her for 18 years," "You should be happy for him," "Just keep busy," or "You'll get over it."

• The basic message is: it's not OK to grieve or, especially, express your grief after a child leaves home.

• Let me reassure you that your grief is both normal and necessary. It's just that our culture misunderstands the role of pain and suffering, so many people are contaminated by common misconceptions about grief and mourning.

• Try to find people who will listen without judging or feeling the need to offer overly simple, clichéd solutions. When you receive glib or judgmental advice, ignore it and allow yourself to grieve and mourn as you need to.

CARPE DIEM

Start an advice collection. Whenever someone offers you a quip about children leaving home—good or bad, jot it down. At some point, compare notes with another empty nester or your partner.

30.

GIVE YOUR CHILD SOME SPACE

*"Too often we give children answers to remember
rather than problems to solve."*
— Robert A. Heinlein

- While it may not always look that way, our children are trying to figure out how to become adults. That is a developmental task that they need to do without us.

- Close your eyes and think back to when you were 17 or 18 or 20. What were you doing? How did you spend your time? What did you care the most about?

- Are you there? Are you inhabiting your young-adult self? Good. Now ask: how focused on your parents were you at that age?

- Except in unusual circumstances (such as a sick mother or father), young adults are usually not focused on their parents. Instead, they're consumed with getting started on their own lives. They may be adults, but they're immature ones. And the only way to grow into their maturity is to get out there and start making their own choices.

- Often the most loving thing we can do for our newly independent children is to leave them alone, to get out of their way. And the most loving thing we can do for ourselves as we experience the void created by their absence? Grieve and mourn openly and fully.

CARPE DIEM
As hard as it may be, try adopting a policy (at least for the next week
or two) of not being the one to initiate contact with your child.
Let him reach out to you when he needs to.

31.

DECLARE YOUR VALUES

"Your beliefs become your thoughts. Your thoughts become your words. Your words become your actions. Your actions become your habits. Your habits become your values. Your values become your destiny."
— Mahatma Gandhi

- Our values are those things that satisfy us most at our very core. They are our heart's most cherished beliefs and desires.

- Values are different from goals. Goals can be accomplished, checked off the list. Values have to be lived on an ongoing basis. For example, earning your master's degree might be a goal, while to never stop learning might be a value.

- Ask yourself what you value. What makes your life worth living? Which beliefs form the foundation of your life? How does your adult child fit into your list of values? How can you build a new form of relationship with your child based on your values?

- Note that values are often not easy to live by. They tend to require ongoing effort, perseverance, and even courage.

CARPE DIEM
Talk to someone about your most cherished beliefs and desires today.

32.

NOTICE FIVE THINGS

"When you are here and now, not jumping ahead, the miracle has happened. To be in the moment is the miracle."

— Osho

- Honing your ability to live in the moment will help you not only be present to your necessary grief but also identify what really matters to you. And figuring out what matters most will help you live fully the remainder of your precious days.

- One way to work on living in the moment is an exercise called "notice five things." When you're feeling stressed or distracted, stop whatever it is you're doing. Still yourself. Take five deep, slow, in-and-out breaths. Now look around you. Silently name five things you can see. Next name five things you can hear. Then name five things you can feel inside or outside your body. Then name five things you can smell. Even if you're not actively eating or drinking, if you try you can probably name several lingering tastes in your mouth.

- After you're done noticing five things, take a temperature on your thoughts and emotions. Has your anxiety dissipated a little? Are you feeling a bit more centered and calm?

- As parents, we're trained to be constantly thinking of five (or ten or a hundred!) different things that need doing or remembering. Now we have the opportunity to retrain our brains to find fulfillment and peace in the simplicity of the present moment. What a relief to be able to relinquish the tyranny of the monkey mind.

CARPE DIEM
Right now, notice five things.

33.

PRACTICE SPONTANEITY

*"To be more childlike, you don't have to give up being an adult. The
fully integrated person is capable of being both an adult and a child
simultaneously. Recapture the childlike feelings of wide-eyed excitement,
spontaneous appreciation, cutting loose, and being full of awe and
wonder at this magnificent universe."*
— Wayne Dyer

- How's that for an oxymoron—practicing spontaneity! But for us
  parents, who've had to be utterly responsible for many years and put
  the needs of our children before our own, embracing spontaneity
  again can be disconcerting. We need to give ourselves permission to be
  spontaneous. And yes, we may even need to intentionally practice it!

- Now that your nest is emptying, you're probably finding that you have
  a great deal more free time than you used to have. Grocery shopping,
  cooking, laundry, errands, scheduling, household paperwork—lots of
  day-to-day demands have probably eased up. How will you use the
  extra time?

- Whenever you find yourself at loose ends, consciously turn away from
  whatever it is you normally do to kill time (surf the web, watch TV,
  etc.) and turn toward spontaneity. Ask yourself, "What do I really, truly
  feel like doing right now?" Learning to re-attune to your own inner
  spark will probably take time and practice, but it's worth it because it's
  where joy lies.

- Make a spontaneity jar. Write ideas for activities you enjoy or that
  interest you on small slips of paper and keep them in a jar. You might
  want to invite your partner or a close friend to add ideas too. Whenever
  you have some free time, pull a random idea from the jar and go do it!

CARPE DIEM
Start a spontaneity jar or list today.

34.

FIND WAYS TO COPE
WITH THE LONELINESS

*"Language has created the word 'loneliness' to express the pain
of being alone. And it has created the word 'solitude' to
express the glory of being alone."*
— Paul Tillich

- Parents who regularly spent time with their teenage children often find themselves experiencing loneliness when the children leave home.

- This is normal. Any time someone who provided us with companionship is gone from our daily lives, we're bound to feel lonely in those moments that we're newly alone. Embracing our grief over the loneliness is part of our task here. We acknowledge it, we feel it, and we mourn it by expressing it in some way.

- Finding new forms of companionship and community is also part of our task here. Pets, houseguests, foreign exchange students—there are many ways to bring more love into our empty homes. My wife and I feel like we have come full circle. We started with our dogs before we had kids, and now have the daily companionship of our dogs again after the kids left home.

- At the same time, we can also begin to learn how to be content— happy, even—when our children have left the nest. After all, we raised them to launch them.

CARPE DIEM
Make a list of relationships you can build so you'll have people to turn to when you're feeling lonely. Consider whether you want new people or pets in your home.

35.

BE ON THE WATCH FOR OLD GRIEFS

"Life seems sometimes like nothing more than a series of losses, from beginning to end. That's the given. How you respond to those losses, what you make of what's left, that's the part you have to make up as you go."
— Katharine Weber

- Whenever we experience a significant loss, all the other important losses in our lives can be dredged up again. Our children leaving might conjure memories and feelings we associate with other losses we've experienced, such as deaths or divorce.

- Don't be surprised if you find yourself thinking about other painful times in your life and feeling emotions you thought were long since spent.

- Find someone to talk to about the pain. A friend who can listen without judging or feeling the need to fix your problems is the best helper you could have right now.

- If you have significant old griefs that you've never truly mourned, now is a good time to see a grief counselor. You might well be carrying accumulated grief, and the compassionate support of a professional counselor may be just what you need to finally confront and embrace the pain so that it can stop suppressing your divine spark and holding you back.

CARPE DIEM

Name the three most significant losses in your life so far. Spend a few minutes thinking about and feeling whether you've fully mourned them.

36.

KNOW THAT YOUR BODY WILL GRIEVE TOO

"Every day you should reach out and touch someone.
People love a warm hug, or just a friendly pat on the back."
— Maya Angelou

- Parenting is very physical. When our kids are little, there's lots of holding and carrying and feeding and diapering, not to mention birthing and breastfeeding! As the children grow, our bodies remain in constant motion, it seems, because they still need daily meals, laundry, chauffeuring, help with activities, and hugs.

- But now that the house is empty, our bodies can suffer. First, our grief can cause feelings of anxiety and depression, which manifest themselves in our bodies. We might feel lethargic, and we might have trouble sleeping. We might also experience muscle aches and pains, feelings of emptiness in our stomachs or tightness in our throats, heart palpitations, headaches, changes in appetite, and other physical symptoms.

- What's more, our bodies miss the activity and physical contact of caring for children. What are our bodies supposed to do now?

- Good self-care is essential. Resting, eating well, drinking enough water, and regular exercise will help us feel better. And finding new outlets and activities for our bodies is also important.

CARPE DIEM
Make an appointment with your healthcare provider for a checkup.

37.

GIVE YOURSELF TIME

"Where you used to be, there is a hole in the world, which I find myself constantly walking around in the daytime, and falling in at night. I miss you like hell."
— Edna St. Vincent Millay

- Grief takes time. Depending on your unique circumstances, such as the number of children you have and how much time might elapse from the day your first child takes steps toward independence until the day your last child is fully on her own, you may experience different phases of empty-nester grief over many years.

- Even if you have one child taking flight, don't expect to integrate your empty-nester grief in a few weeks or months. The truth is that we don't truly get over grief. Instead, we learn to live with it. We learn to integrate our losses into our ongoing lives. And even then we have pangs of grief forever. I like to call these "griefbursts."

- Be patient with yourself. Be patient with your child. Be patient with your partner and other family members. All of you are moving through a challenging, extended process.

- Whatever you do, don't set a timetable for your healing. Just trust that if you keep working on the six needs of mourning (Ideas 6 to 11), you're moving toward finding a new and rewarding equilibrium.

CARPE DIEM

In a notebook or journal, note today's date, then write about how you're feeling. Months from now you'll be able to look back on what you wrote and see that even though it doesn't feel like it some days, you're making progress.

38.

GO OFF THE DEEP END

"There is a time for extravagant gestures. There is a time to pour out your affections on one you love. And when the time comes, seize it."
— Max Lucado

- Becoming an empty nester can feel like plunging into a cold, deep sea. All at once, we're somewhere foreign and uncomfortable.

- Sometimes when we experience a major transition, we feel the need to respond with equally large gestures. It can seem like Newton's third law of motion—for every action there must be an equal and opposite reaction.

- Sometimes a few little crying jags won't do it, for example. We need to sob uncontrollably for days. Or we need to do something else that feels Big, like take a major vacation or...I don't know...buy a boat!

- I'm certainly not condoning overly rash, irresponsible, or unsafe behavior here, but I do want to affirm that if you feel like making a grand gesture of some kind when your child leaves home, you're not alone. It's a natural response, and one you may want to choose to indulge.

CARPE DIEM

Feeling the need to make a grand gesture? Float the idea with someone you know to be both reasonable and compassionate. And if you have a partner, don't forget to run it by him or her.

39.

BE AWARE OF "BORROWED TEARS"

"It's so curious: one can resist tears in the hardest hours of grief. But then someone makes you a friendly sign behind a window, or one notices that a flower that was in bud only yesterday has suddenly blossomed, or a letter slips from a drawer…and everything collapses."
— Colette

- Have you found yourself easily choked up or weepy since your child began to take flight? Maybe you started crying when you saw a school bus or watched a sappy TV commercial? If so, you may be experiencing what I call "borrowed tears."

- Borrowed tears seem to come out of nowhere and are triggered by something you don't necessarily associate with your child moving out and wouldn't normally have been upset by. You're crying because your heart and soul are hurting and your emotions are tender.

- Think of it this way: If you press on your leg gently with your hand, it doesn't hurt. But if you sprain your ankle and then press on it, even the slightest touch can hurt. Your heart is sprained right now, and anything that touches it even slightly may hurt. This is normal and will pass as your heart continues to heal.

CARPE DIEM
The next time you find yourself feeling weepy, surrender to the tears.
Cry as long and as hard as you feel like.

40.

ACKNOWLEDGE YOUR GRIEF OVER YOUR OWN AGING

---

*"The afternoon of life is just as full as the morning;
only its meaning and purposes are different."*
— Carl Jung

- Part of our empty-nest grief, of course, is our thoughts and feelings about our own aging.

- Our children becoming adults signals to us that we, too, are entering a new phase of life. We're now middle-aged. We might even be considered "seniors." And grandkids? They could be on the way at any time!

- It's normal to grieve over aging. After all, we're experiencing new age-related losses all the time. Our bodies are morphing. Our minds aren't as sharp as they used to be. Our social lives and family relationships are changing as well. We have fewer and fewer days to look forward to here on earth.

- Your grief over aging is probably intertwined with your empty-nester grief right now, and that's OK. It's not necessary to sort the symptoms into two piles, like laundry. Just dump the whole mess into the mourning machine. It will help you with both.

CARPE DIEM
Talk to someone today about your empty-nesting and aging grief, preferably someone who can relate to both.

41.

SEEK HELP IF YOU MAY BE CLINICALLY DEPRESSED

"There is no need to suffer silently, and there is no shame in seeking help."
— Joel S. Manuel

- Sadness is a hallmark symptom of grief. When we're grieving, it's normal to feel sad.

- Sadness forces us to regroup—physically, cognitively, emotionally, socially, and spiritually. When we are sad, we instinctively turn inward. We withdraw. We slow down. It's as if our soul presses the pause button and says, "Whoa, whoa, whoaaa. Time out. I need to acknowledge what's happened here and really consider what I want to do next."

- But sometimes the natural and necessary sadness of empty-nester grief can grow into clinical depression. If your grief is preventing you from completing daily tasks (such as hygiene, work, errands, participating in routine family time), and/or if you are challenged by ongoing feelings of worthlessness, hopelessness, or suicidal thoughts, these are signs that you might be suffering from clinical depression.

- If you or others see these signs in you, make an appointment with your mental health caregiver or primary care physician right away. Talk therapy, medication, or a combination of the two can do wonders to ease your suffering and help you get back on track.

CARPE DIEM
If you may be clinically depressed, call today to make an appointment with your primary caregiver.

42.

CREATE NEW WAYS OF CONNECTING

*"Stay committed to your decisions, but stay flexible
in your approach. It's the end you're after."*
— Anthony Robbins

- Some of the ways in which you've always connected with your child may now have to be adapted or changed altogether. After all, you're no longer under the same roof. You might not even be in the same state or country.

- Mourning the loss of cherished routines is part of your work now. If you're sad that you can no longer have dinner together every night or watch a certain TV show with one another, allow yourself to be sad. Embrace the pain and remember. Send a text or email letting your child know that you're missing her in that moment, and talk about your feelings with your partner or a friend.

- Even as you're mourning, though, you can simultaneously work to build new ways of connecting. I don't know about your kids, but mine are OK with occasional texts or phone calls from me. Family vacations are still welcome, though it's increasingly difficult to find a time that works for everyone. Small, random kindnesses can have a big impact. Send a written note in the mail. Ship a token gift.

- If your child still comes home occasionally, on weekends or holidays, create new rituals that fit his schedule and current likes. Make their favorite biscuits and gravy or go for a hike. Combine a shopping trip for necessities with dinner and a movie. If your child can't make it home very often, schedule a weekly phone call. And go to him. Make an occasional visit to your child's home a top priority. Start a new tradition of spending certain holidays together. Our family enjoys getting together for Thanksgiving in Arizona. Long-distance relationships need regular face-to-face time to stay meaningful.

CARPE DIEM
Make plans today for the next time of connection you'll have with
your child. Be realistic. Shoot for a focused hour or two instead
of a whole weekend, for example.

43.

EXPLORE ANY REGRETS

"No parent is perfect; we all can look back and think of things we could've done to help our children be better prepared for adulthood. And sometimes it's best to admit it to them and encourage them to learn from our mistakes."
— Billy Graham

- I don't know about you, but I haven't been a perfect parent. I did the best I knew how to do, but still I have some regrets.

- Any parenting regrets you may have are part of your empty-nester grief. Like any grief thought or feeling you experience, they need exploring and expressing.

- Talk about your regrets with your partner or a friend. If your own parents are still alive, you might consider sharing your regrets with them. Chances are, such an intergenerational discussion could result in healing affirmation and insight.

- Share your regrets with your child. If you feel sorry about something, apologize. Say, "I just wanted to let you know that I'm sorry that…" If your regrets have to do with circumstances you can still change, then make a plan to change them, and share this plan with your child. On the other hand, don't over-project your regrets onto your child. Sharing them with a trusted friend or counselor may be enough.

- The bottom line is that while humans are imperfect, if we're aware of and open about our shortcomings, and if we work to transcend them, we're modeling good self-responsibility for our children. We're also strengthening our relationships and growing as individuals—two of the most important things in life.

CARPE DIEM
Talk about your parenting regrets with someone you trust.
Consider if you want to communicate your feelings of regret to
your child, and if so, how to do it.

44.

ALLOW FOR RESENTMENT

"Where there is anger, there is always pain underneath."
— Eckhart Tolle

• It's normal for grieving empty nesters to experience a wide range of emotions. This may include feelings of resentment or envy.

• If, thanks to your hard work, your children are experiencing privileges you were not able to at their age, this can stir mixed feelings. You might feel pride and happiness as well as resentment.

• College costs and children's living expenses can be extremely burdensome. If you are sacrificing or strapping yourself financially to support your child, it's also understandable for this to rankle, especially if you feel your child is taking it for granted.

• Remember that feelings aren't good or bad—they just are. This includes feelings of anger or resentment. Try talking out your resentment with your partner, a friend, or a counselor. See if you can get to the core of your feelings; they may be rooted in your own childhood. Also try to separate such feelings from circumstances within your child's control. You may be mixing up resentment over circumstances with resentment toward your child.

• As a young adult, your child needs to learn about adult realities. It's appropriate to have budget discussions with your child, for example, and to create real-world limits and expectations. It's not appropriate to blame or shame.

CARPE DIEM
If you're feeling any envy or resentment, talk to someone about it today.

45.

PUT PLANS ON THE CALENDAR

"Never, ever underestimate the importance of having fun."
— Randy Pausch

- We all need things to look forward to.

- In the midst of your empty-nester grief, it might help you to have special plans on the calendar—a vacation, a visit to distant relatives, a concert or other event, a day-trip with your child.

- Colleges have parent weekends in the fall for just this reason. They know that after children have been gone from home for a couple of months, it's time for a reunion. By then, parents and kids alike are looking forward to spending a day or two together. My wife and I made it a point to visit our kids at university, creating long-lasting memories.

- Official parent weekend or not, you can make whatever plans you'd like to visit your child, or vice versa. It could even be a recurring event, like brunch the first Sunday of every month or a series of hikes or 5K races. I've found there's something very special about visiting your kids in their new or temporary homes, whether they're at college, living and working in a new city, studying abroad, etc.

CARPE DIEM
Make plans to see your child sometime in the next month or two.

46.

REBUILD FRIENDSHIPS

"It takes a long time to grow an old friend."
— John Leonard

- It's common today for parents' friendships to slide. Once our kids are in school and start getting involved in activities, we're so busy chauffeuring them, helping them with homework, and attending their games, performances, and parties that we often lose touch with our own social networks.

- Now that you've got some time back, reconnecting with friends is a wise investment. If you haven't touched base much, that first contact might feel a little awkward, but do it anyway. Better to have reached out and been embarrassed than never to have reached out at all.

- We need friends in the last third of our lives just as much as we needed them in earlier years. Maybe more so, actually. Researchers call our ties of trust, connection, and participation "social capital." Studies show the higher seniors' social capital, the better their physical, cognitive, and emotional well-being.

- Call an old friend today. Set a date to have coffee or dinner out. If you and your partner have "couples friends," start rebuilding those relationships too. Reach out to neighbors and work buddies. And of course, make new friends when the opportunity presents itself!

CARPE DIEM
Reach out to an old friend today.

47.

RECOMMIT TO (OR RETHINK) YOUR PARTNER

*"A successful marriage requires falling in love many times,
always with the same person."*
— Mignon McLaughlin

- The empty-nest transition is a time to take stock of your life. This includes your relationship with your partner.

- If your relationship is good, and both of you are happy to have it form the foundation of the rest of your years, congratulations. For you, this time is an opportunity to deepen an already strong partnership. Be open about any dissatisfactions. Discuss goals and dreams often. Spend time together as well as apart. Enjoy each other.

- If your relationship is rocky, spend some of your newfound free time figuring out what you want to do. Now may be the moment to recommit to your relationship. Counseling can be just the catalyst you need to work through your challenges and emerge stronger than ever.

- The empty-nest years are also a time when many couples go their separate ways. While the overall divorce rate in the US has fallen since 1990, it has doubled for couples over 50. In fact, one out of three Baby Boomers will be unmarried in older age.

- Whatever your path, choose to take it consciously and on purpose in order to live your remaining years with as much joy and presence as possible.

CARPE DIEM
Take your partner out to lunch or dinner today.
Discuss whatever's most pressing on your minds and hearts.

48.

PRACTICE LIVING IN THE NOW

"Nothing has happened in the past; it happened in the Now. Nothing will ever happen in the future; it will happen in the Now."

— Eckhart Tolle

- We feel our grief over our children's departure in the now. Our hearts ache; our throats clench. We experience the lack of their presence in the now. We miss them in the now.

- But we also spend a great deal of time worrying about the future without them. What will we do? How will we fill our days? When will we see them next?

- It's normal to wonder and worry, but it's also healthy to bring ourselves back to the now. Where are you? What is around you? Who is near you? How does your body feel? What do you hear? What do you taste? What do you smell?

- The next time your grief takes you into Worryland, try refocusing your attention on the here and now. Put yourself in a physical situation that you find soothing, such as a hot bath, a walk outdoors on a sunny day, or a rest on the couch with a blanket, a cup of tea, and a good book. Be where you are, and trust that the future will work itself out when it, too, is the Now.

CARPE DIEM
Return yourself to the now with the breathing exercise in Idea 5.

49.

REACQUAINT YOURSELF WITH YOU

"At the center of your being, you have the answer; you know who you are, and you know what you want."
— Lao Tzu

- We've already talked about your need to create a new self-identity (Idea 9). Here I'd like to offer some suggested ways to move that needle.

- Think back to the things you were passionate about as a child or young teen. It's thought that childhood obsessions are often "true," unadulterated callings. Some empty nesters find threads that they would like to pick up again. I myself first became excited about the idea of grief counseling when I was 14, and it's still the fire that lights my candle today. My wife, Sue, has always loved to travel. Now that she has more time, she runs a women's travel club. Since I travel so much for my work, I'm content staying home while she and her friends explore the world.

- Take a few continuing education classes. More than 100 colleges around the country have a program called the Osher Lifelong Learning Institute, which offers low-cost classes on myriad topics to community members. Your local library, community college, and senior center are other organizations that provide workshops, seminars, and courses. Exposing yourself to new ideas and people will stimulate your creativity.

- Ask the people who know you best. Your lifelong friends, your current besties, and your partner will all have answers to the question, "What do you think I would enjoy doing now?" Their insights just might reveal a path that you weren't aware of.

CARPE DIEM
Today, talk to a couple of the people who know you best.
Ask them what they think you should do with your new free time.
Don't judge their answers; just listen and gather.

50.

UNDERSTAND THE DIFFERENCE BETWEEN CLEAN AND DIRTY PAIN

"Imaginary obstacles are insurmountable. Real ones aren't. But you can't tell the difference when you have no real information. Fear can create even more imaginary obstacles than ignorance can. That's why the smallest step away from speculation and into reality can be an amazing relief."

— Barbara Sher

- The fear of our empty-nester grief can be crippling. It's natural to worry—about how we'll go on, about how our child is doing, about what will happen next. But sometimes the worry looms too large. It takes over, rendering us incapable of feeling or doing anything else.

- Usually when fear and worry are dominating, it's because we're suffering from "dirty pain." "Clean pain" is the normal pain that follows difficult life experiences. "Dirty pain" is the damaging, multiplied pain we create when we catastrophize, judge ourselves, or allow ourselves to be judged by others.

- Dirty pain is the story we tell ourselves about the clean pain. Dirty pain is the imaginary obstacles we put in our own way. For example, "I miss my child tonight" is clean pain. "She probably won't even want to come home next summer" is dirty pain. Our worries about the future are dirty pain.

- Recognizing dirty pain helps us banish it, as does actively seeking the truth if we are assuming something terrible.

CARPE DIEM
Today, talk to someone about something that's been bothering you. Seek to understand whether it's clean pain or dirty pain.

51.

MAKE TIME FOR SPIRITUALITY

"We are not human beings on a spiritual journey.
We are spiritual beings on a human journey."
— Stephen R. Covey

- All grief is, at bottom, a spiritual quest. At times of transition and loss, we naturally ponder life's biggest questions. Why are we here? Why does everyone we love have to get older and change? What will give my life meaning from here forward?

- Actively working on our spirituality helps us not only move toward answers to these important questions but also live with a deeper sense of peace and fulfillment. Along the way, we move through our grief and learn to reconcile ourselves to it.

- Make time for spiritual practice every day. Just like brushing your teeth and exercising, spiritual habits are essential self-care. Some people meditate. Others pray, do yoga, attend a place of worship, or read a spiritual text such as the Bible.

- If you're not in the spiritual habit already, take steps toward it. Try out different places of worship and daily practices. Find something that makes your soul sing.

CARPE DIEM
Spend at least ten minutes attending to your spirituality today.

52.

LEVERAGE TECHNOLOGY

"Smart phones and social media expand our universe. We can connect with others or collect information easier and faster than ever."
— Daniel Goleman

- If you're not using social media and your children are, I recommend you climb aboard. Yes, it can be tricky to navigate what's appropriate for whom, but the bottom line is that social media is a great way to stay abreast of the day-to-day activities of people you care about but can't spend time with often.

- Ask your kids which social media tools they're using and think you should start with. My own kids use Instagram, Snapchat, and Skype. They stay in touch with me through texting and email.

- Apart from social media, there are lots of technology tools that can help you stay in touch with your kids. Texting, of course, is almost universally popular. Emails and blogging are great. Snapchat is a smart phone app that lets you send and receive photos and short video clips, which then disappear. Skype, Google Hangouts, and other video-calling apps approximate talking face-to-face.

- Don't forget online games! The back-and-forth of Words with Friends, for instance, can help you feel connected day-by-day even if you're not talking or sharing news daily.

CARPE DIEM
Learn a new technology trick today.

53.

MAKE FRIENDS WITH THE EMPTY BEDROOM

"An empty room is a story waiting to happen, and you are the author."
— Charlotte Moss

- Each of my three children had their own bedroom, so when, one at a time, they left home for college, their rooms grew suddenly silent. For a long time, I always felt pangs of grief when I walked by their open doors and saw how spare and lifeless the rooms now seemed.

- If you feel similar pangs of grief over the empty bedroom, take them as an invitation to mourn. Walk into the bedroom. Sit on the bed and remember your child. Cry if you feel like crying. Don't treat the bedroom like a "do not enter" zone. Avoiding the room is avoiding your grief.

- Talk to your child and the rest of your family about what, if anything, to do with the empty room. If there's no rush, don't rush. If your child will be returning to use the bedroom on weekends and holidays, it's usually best to let it remain his, if possible. But you might want to take advantage of its availability to spruce it up while he's gone. Painting and redecorating a bit can ready the room for guests.

- Even if it remains her bedroom, maybe you would like to start turning it into a multi-purpose space, such as for exercise, crafting, or another hobby you've long neglected. Doing so will help you take steps toward creating your new self-identity and realizing you are experiencing a new phase of life's journey.

CARPE DIEM
Hang out in the empty bedroom for a while today. See what comes up.

54.

BELIEVE IN THE POWER OF "AND"

"It kills you to see them grow up.
But I guess it would kill you quicker if they didn't."
— Barbara Kingsolver

- We empty-nester parents often feel ambivalent. The word "ambivalence" comes from *ambi*, which means "two," and *valence*, which means "feeling." Ambivalence means to feel two opposing ways at the same time.

- When our children begin to take flight, we're excited for them and for ourselves, and we're sad and in grief over the losses the child's departure from our daily lives will bring.

- That little "and" I placed in the last sentence holds remarkable power. In fact, it may be the whole key to not only surviving but thriving through the empty-nester years. We must mourn *and* celebrate. We must feel loss *and* hope.

- Whenever you're feeling deeply blue, try to call to mind the power of "and." Your natural sadness is necessary, it's true, but even in the midst of your sadness you can also conjure humor, excitement, and hope. With empty-nester grief, especially, it's good sense to work toward having it both ways.

CARPE DIEM
Complete this sentence: Today I feel _____
and _____. Now go talk about it
with someone who cares about you.

55.

PRACTICE THINKING, "I WANT..."

"Everything you want is out there waiting for you to ask. Everything you want also wants you. But you have to take action to get it."
— Jack Canfield

- Parents usually subordinate their own needs to their children's. The children's needs come first, and only after those are met do the parents get to consider their own. But by then all the time, energy, and money are often used up, so parents may end up deferring their own wants for years, until after the children leave home.

- Because of this phenomenon, you might be out of practice even thinking about what you want, let alone acting on it. Now that you've finally reached the empty-nesting years, though, it's time to reacquaint yourself with you.

- What do you want? What do you want today? What do you want this weekend? What are some big things you want? What are some small things you'd love to do or have? Sue and I have decided we want to travel more to warm places during the winter months. We eventually want time with grandchildren—but we're not in a hurry!

- Equally important questions to start asking: What don't you want? Where do you want? Why do you want? Who do you want?

CARPE DIEM
Make a list of "I wants." Then make a list of "I don't wants."

56.

RENEW INTIMACY

"Intimacy is not purely physical. It's the act of connecting with someone so deeply, you feel like you can see into their soul."

— Greg Friedman

- If your house is empty of children now, and it's just you and your partner, it's time to reignite the flame, right? Maybe…but it's often not that simple.

- How many years has it been since you could freely focus on one another's physical needs, without having to worry about children bursting into your room or listening from down the hall? 20? 30? That's a long time.

- A lot has changed since you were young lovers. Your bodies are different now. Your relationship is different now. Your needs are different now.

- If your sex life is already solid, it's still a good time to check in with your partner. Talk openly about what each of you envisions and hopes for now that the children are leaving home.

- If your sex life needs attention, try starting with a conversation outside the bedroom. A moonlit walk or car ride might be a good venue. Be honest and loving. And discuss how your empty-nester grief and age-related changes may be affecting your sex drive.

- Empty-nester partners who have grown apart often need to renew other facets of their relationship before they can revive physical intimacy. Communication and finding new mutual interests are key first steps on the road to reigniting the flame.

CARPE DIEM
Give your partner a neck-and-shoulders massage today.

57.

CONSIDER YOUR CAREER

"Never continue in a job you don't enjoy. If you're happy in what you're doing, you'll like yourself, you'll have inner peace. And if you have that, along with physical health, you will have had more success than you could possibly have imagined."

— Johnny Carson

- Do you love your job? Are you crazy about your career? If the answer is "no," it's not too late to rethink the remainder of your working years.

- Make an appointment with a career counselor. She'll help you consider your options. You can also take a free online career aptitude test.

- If you feel stuck, maybe the immediate goal is simply to feel motion. Talk to your supervisor or HR person about other roles in your company. Take a class after work that helps you learn more about your dream career. Read a book about changing jobs in mid-life. Add a volunteer gig to your plate. If you are fortunate, maybe you can afford to retire and pursue other interests. If so, count your blessings.

- Life is short, my friend. I hope you will spend the rest of your precious days doing something for which you feel you have a true calling or passion.

CARPE DIEM
Take one small step today toward aligning your career with your calling.

58.

BUILD NEW COMMUNITIES

"In most vital organizations, there is a common bond of interdependence, mutual interest, interlocking contributions, and simple joy."
— Max DePree

- We as human beings are built to interact with one another. We exist in relation to other people. So essential are relationships that studies of prisoners in solitary confinement show profound and long-term psychological damage.

- When we became parents, we also became a part of many new communities. The pediatrician's practice. Preschool. Soccer team. Perhaps a new neighborhood. Followed by elementary school, Cub Scouts, gymnastics, theater… You get my drift.

- Our children's communities kept us busy and socially involved. Now that we're no longer part of many of these groups, it's time to connect with new communities.

- Find a new organization or group to be a part of. Consider a group connected to one of your passions or to a cause you support. Volunteering is also a great way to find community.

- Don't make the mistake of thinking you don't need community. You do. Simplifying is often good, but isolating is not. People who stay socially connected are happier, healthier, and even live longer.

CARPE DIEM
Inquire or make overtures to connect to a new community today.

59.

RECONSIDER THE "EMPTY" IN "EMPTY NEST"

"I ponder the rhythms of letting go and embracing whatever is around the corner, trusting that the empty spaces will be filled. And knowing that sometimes community can happen only in the gaps where mystery resides."
— Joyce Hollyday

- It's funny how we think of our nests as empty after our children leave. Before they came along, our homes were full of love and activity, weren't they? We had our own lives, maybe a partner, a number of friends, perhaps a pet or two. My wife and I had Siberian huskies before we had children. What did you have?

- Of course, our children filled our homes and our days to overflowing. But now that they're off starting their own adventures and our homes and lives feel "empty," we can choose to befriend the emptiness in several ways.

- Some among us revel in the quiet of the empty. While we still grieve for our missing children, we enjoy the solitude and peace.

- Others among us take this opportunity to downsize. We acknowledge the empty, and we choose to progress to smaller, more simple lives. Having simplified, we are free to travel more.

- Still others of us acknowledge the empty and then fill it. We hearken back to our pre-child days. We turn our homes into Airbnbs. We invite out-of-town friends to visit. We foster pets. We host dinner parties and holiday celebrations.

CARPE DIEM
Today, give some thought to the emptiness and what you might want to do about it when you're ready.

60.

THINK MOMENTUM

"Getting over a painful experience is much like crossing monkey bars.
You have to let go at some point in order to move forward."
— C.S. Lewis

- Mourning is grief in motion. Mourning is taking our internal thoughts and feelings about our child's departure and giving them movement by actively expressing them in some way.

- While we don't actually "get over" or "let go" of our losses, we can use the image of the monkey bars to help us remember to keep doing the hard work of moving.

- Movement softens grief. Grief in motion is grief that has momentum toward healing.

- Whenever you're feeling stuck or in despair, think momentum. Ask yourself, "How can I give this thought or feeling motion?"

- Momentum doesn't mean denying, going around, or hurrying up. It does mean encountering, exploring, naming, befriending, and sharing.

CARPE DIEM

What's your most prominent thought or feeling of empty-nester grief today? Give it motion by expressing it outside of yourself somehow today.

61.

ASK YOURSELF: WHAT GIVES ME JOY?

"It's a helluva start, being able to recognize what makes you happy."
— Lucille Ball

- In other Ideas in this book, we've talked about relearning to identify your own wants again and moving your long back-burnered hopes and dreams to the front burner. Those are the hard-won rewards of empty nesting.

- But the essence of a life well-lived from here forward comes from regularly and honestly engaging with this single question: what gives me joy?

- As parents, we found joy in raising our children. While it certainly wasn't easy or heartache-free, we understood that our love for and relationships with our children made everything worth it. In fact, the challenges are what made the contrasting joys knowable. Now we need to pay attention to what gives us joy from moment-to-moment in the dailyness of life without children.

- What gives you that warm, contented feeling of joy? Probably a number of things. Going for a walk? Puttering around in the garage? Petting your dog? Helping someone else? Holding your beloved's hand? Singing? Making something? Continuing to enjoy your work life? Traveling somewhere new? However you find joy, seek to do more and more of that, and let everything else fall by the wayside.

CARPE DIEM
Make a conscious effort to do seven (yes, seven!)
little things that give you joy today.

62.

BE GRATEFUL FOR YOUR GRIEF

"One word frees us of all the weight and pain of life: that word is love."
— Sophocles

- "You are loved, and your purpose is to love," said spiritual mentor Marianne Williamson. In grief we realize that this is the Catch-22 of life.

- Love is the most joyous and meaningful experience there is. Love gives our lives purpose. But love's conjoined twin is grief. If we love, we will eventually grieve.

- So what is there to do but continue loving? When we express our ongoing love for our child who has moved on, we are mourning and moving toward healing. When we embrace the love of others, we are accepting the balm of grace and healing. If we shun or hide ourselves from love, on the other hand, we are choosing to die while we are alive.

- Love, then, is not just the best answer—it is the only answer. If we're grateful for the love we have been able to share with our child, we must also be grateful for the grief.

CARPE DIEM

Write your grief a letter today. "Dear grief…" Tell it what you're thinking and feeling, what has surprised you most, what you're struggling with, and what your intentions are for the future.

63.

CELEBRATE YOUR HERITAGE

*"We inherit from our ancestors gifts so often taken for granted.
Each of us contains within this inheritance of soul. We are links
between the ages, containing past and present expectations,
sacred memories, and future promise."*
— Edward Sellner

- As we've already discussed, part of what makes the empty-nest transition so difficult is the movement into the next phase of our own lives. Simply put, we're getting older. That's part of our grief and our need to mourn.

- But let's not minimize the accomplishment that comes with aging, either. If we are moving into our third act, that's a remarkable milestone. And if our own parents are still alive, they are likely moving into their fourth and final act. But that does not mean that their lives are any less valuable, does it?

- Empty nesting is a good time to research and celebrate your heritage. You are part of a long, long line of ancestors, and with any luck you will be followed by a long, long line of offspring. Seeing yourself and your brief but unique life in the context of your family's entire history can be both interesting and humbling.

- I have found that our adult children usually get interested in genealogy eventually. Recording your family's heritage in a form you can pass along to them is a gift they will treasure down the line. Maybe you and your adult child can even travel to your family's birthplace together one day.

CARPE DIEM
Try a free trial at Ancestry.com and see what you can learn
in a few short searches.

64.

START NEW TRADITIONS

"Rituals give kids a sense of security in a fast-moving,
unpredictable world, as well as memories they will cherish a lifetime."
— Betsy Taylor

- Families are held together not only by love but by routines and traditions. The feeling of "home" comes, in part, from knowing that certain things are always done a certain way and that you can count on the people and the place always being there.

- Now that your family members are starting to go their separate ways, it's time to think about starting new traditions and rituals. While your old rituals might continue to be cherished for holidays and special family gatherings, you can also create new rituals for other occasions.

- Think about the regular routines that held your family together. Did you have dinner together every night? A movie on Fridays? A regular visit to a place of worship, library, park, or restaurant? What new routines can you now substitute for those? For example, depending on your distance from one another, maybe you could Skype every Saturday morning or commit to getting together face-to-face once a month or once every other month.

- Realize that your adult children might resist initiating new traditions. My own still want to gather for Christmas in the home they grew up in. It's nice that they have the instinct to retain this routine, yet my wife and I will probably want to make a change at some point in time.

CARPE DIEM
Brainstorm ideas for new family traditions.

65.

SPEND YOUR PRECIOUS TIME ON WHAT REALLY MATTERS

"The proper function of man is to live, not to exist. I shall not waste my days in trying to prolong them. I shall use my time."
— Jack London

- When our children move on, we begin to become more aware of the fleeting nature of life. The time went so fast, and now we have less than half our lives left.

- This new awareness of the preciousness of time is something we can grab hold of and wring for all it's worth. In other words, from here forward we can really strive to live the wisdom it offers.

- In your daily life, what do you do that really matters to you? What do you spend time on that doesn't? Work to spend more of your time on the former and less on the latter—and watch your quality of life go up.

- Start with some low-hanging fruit. If you tend to spend your evenings in front of the TV or surfing the internet, for example, ask yourself if you would feel more fulfilled swapping out some of that time for something more meaningful.

CARPE DIEM
Today, swap out half an hour of blah, wasted time for something you find more meaningful.

66.

TAKE LESSONS

"Anyone who keeps learning stays young."
— Henry Ford

- When we want to get better at a particular skill and would benefit from mentoring and structure, we take lessons.

- We tend to think of lesson-taking as the province of young people, but I'd like to encourage us to shift our thinking: lessons are a privilege of age. After all, we're experienced enough now to know what we're interested in and what we're not. We have free time, and we might have some extra pocket change. Plus, we've earned it!

- What's great about lessons is that the teaching is often one-on-one. We get to learn firsthand, up close and personal, from a seasoned journeyman, often in the comfort of our own home.

- You can take lessons in just about anything you can imagine, from piano and guitar to foreign languages (Sue recently took up Spanish and Italian), fly fishing, cooking, golf, singing, American Sign Language, horseback riding, you name it. On Craigslist, check out your local list under the heading "lessons and tutoring."

CARPE DIEM
Sign up for a lesson today.

67.

RECONNECT WITH YOUR SIBLINGS

"We know one another's faults, virtues, catastrophes, mortifications, triumphs, rivalries, desires, and how long we can each hang by our hands to a bar. We have been banded together under pack codes and tribal laws."
— Rose Macauley

- A researcher at the University of Indianapolis found that when their children left home, many empty-nester parents not only reformed their relationships with their kids, their partners, and themselves, they also grew closer to their own siblings.

- If you've got time on your hands now, why not reach out to your brothers and sisters? Make a long-overdue visit, or plan a family trip somewhere together. I recently took a week's vacation with my brother.

- In fact, a family reunion might be in order. Call your family member who's best at organizing events and suggest planning a reunion. Offer to be his second-in-command. Or, if this is you, get started with the planning.

- A stay with a sibling who still has kids (or grandkids!) at home allows you to experience the full nest vicariously again. Enjoy your nieces and nephews.

CARPE DIEM
Call a sibling or cousin today.

68.

DANGLE A CARROT

"More flies are caught with honey than with vinegar."
— Proverb

- Twenty-somethings can be notoriously hard for parents to have a relationship with. As I've said, this is normal. Developmentally, our young adult children are learning how to be independent. This means they need us to leave them alone.

- So yes, leave them alone. Let them contact you more than vice versa. Don't pressure them too often about getting together.

- BUT! Now and then, you can also dangle a carrot. If you can afford to, offer to buy a plane ticket if they'll come to visit. Cook their favorite meal and invite them and their friends to dinner. Plan and pay for a family trip that they won't want to miss.

- There's nothing wrong with wanting to keep your family close. Occasional and judiciously dangled carrots can help you do that.

CARPE DIEM
What's a carrot you can dangle to help keep your family close
in the next several months? Start stringing it up today.

69.

FIND THE HUMOR

"Children learn to smile from their parents."
— Shinichi Suzuki

- Life is sad. Life is wonderful. But maybe most of all, life is funny.

- If you think about it, we humans live ridiculous lives. Amazing and terrible things happen around us every day. Sometimes they happen to us. Most of them we can't control.

- I bet some funny things have happened as your child stepped through the process of taking flight. Do you have enough perspective yet to be able to tell the story to someone else and chuckle a bit?

- When you find yourself getting angry or upset about something empty-nest-related, try looking for the humor. What if you were to laugh instead of scream in frustration? Give it a try.

CARPE DIEM
If you find yourself getting angry or upset today,
stop, breathe, and look for the humor.

70.

FIX SOMETHING

*"There are risks and costs to action. But they are far less than the
long-range risks of comfortable inaction."*
— John F. Kennedy

- You know all those little things in our lives that are broken, but we get so used to their brokenness that we barely notice them anymore?

- For example, the door on my Center for Loss kitchen cabinet in which the trashcan is stored has not closed properly for…I bet it's been at least three years. The screw holes near the upper hinge have gotten stripped, and while it's not quite falling off, the door hangs a bit catawampus. Yet my staff and I use it day in and day out, and its ineffectiveness is a daily diminishment.

- It's time for me to fix that cabinet door—or get someone to fix it for me. Inaction weighs us down. Living with brokenness—not putting forth the effort to make it right—dulls and drains us.

- Of course, this rule of thumb applies not just to household or office items but also to relationships, financial issues, and yes, grief. While we can't "fix" our grief, we can and must take action to experience and express it. Ignoring it won't make it go away. Only engaging with it will.

CARPE DIEM
Fix something small today.

71.

WORK THROUGH DASHED EXPECTATIONS OR BROKEN DREAMS

"A very painful part of being a parent is having really negative feelings about your children when you love them so much."
— Louis C.K.

- If your children don't take the path you envisioned for them, or if they're struggling with their adult lives, this will likely compound your natural grief.

- Working through the empty-nest transition also means learning to let go of our attachment to outcome. We can't control our independent children, nor would we want to, not really. Yes, it hurts to see them suffer or fail. And yes, our undying love for them means that when they suffer, we suffer too. But still, their lives are their lives. We must learn to love without trying to control or judge.

- If your grown children are making choices that make you upset or drive you crazy, consider seeing a counselor. A compassionate counselor can help you learn techniques for loving and letting go at the same time.

- Setting incoming boundaries is just as important as setting outgoing boundaries. Deciding how much you will allow your child to impact your life is as necessary as deciding where to draw the line in interfering with your child's life.

CARPE DIEM
Get together with another empty-nester parent and commiserate about dashed expectations and broken dreams. You may be surprised how common the experience is.

72.

EXPAND YOUR LIFE TO INTERSECT WITH YOUR INDEPENDENT CHILD'S

*"If you want to live an extraordinary life,
find out what the ordinary do—and don't do it."*
— Tommy Newberry

- For eighteen-plus years, you and your child have occupied an intimate space together. You have lived in close physical and emotional proximity. But now you're apart. Your child is five, fifty, five hundred, maybe even five thousand miles away from you. How can you possibly bridge that distance?

- One possible way is growth. In other words, you work to grow in order to bridge that distance.

- The more you grow as an individual, the more your life may be able to intersect with your adult child's independent life. Traveling can put you in proximity, of course, but so can learning new skills and meeting new people. The "bigger" your life becomes, the more likely you will be to find things to talk about with your child, uncover shared interests, and plan new adventures together. For example, what might happen if you were to take up long-distance hiking or learn a new language? My wife and older daughter recently walked across England together.

- Of course, seeking to grow will also result in a more fulfilling life for you, period. It just happens to have an extra-special bonus benefit.

CARPE DIEM
Pick something on your "wants" list (Idea 55) that you think might intersect with something on your child's wants list. Start working on it today.

73.

EMPTY THE EMPTY NEST

*"Have nothing in your house that you do not know
to be useful or believe to be beautiful."*
— William Morris

- If you've ever had to clean out a parent's home, you know that there's a fine line between homey and hoarding. In today's abundant world, it's easy to accumulate way too much "stuff." Even those of us who don't think of ourselves as materialists often end up with cabinets and closets chockfull of things we never use. It's just the detritus of decades. And as parents ourselves, well, we often hold onto kid stuff that no one will ever use again.

- The good news is that it's liberating to lighten our surroundings. And I've found that we've often acquired enough discernment by the empty-nest years to be effective in our sorting process. What do we really want, care about, and use? We now understand that it's not ruthless to throw away or donate the rest—it's restorative. While you're at it, ask your adult children to take away anything you might be storing for them.

- Many people have found the book *The Life-Changing Magic of Tidying Up* to be a helpful guide to purging and transforming their homes and even, as the title promises, their lives. Why not give it a try?

- If you can't bring yourself to get started, ask a friend whom you know to be a good organizer to help. Trade for something you're good at—maybe cooking or yard work.

CARPE DIEM
Clean out one drawer or closet today.

74.

SURROUND YOURSELF WITH POSITIVITY

"You are the average of the five people you spend the most time with."
— Jim Rohn

- Are there people in your life whose presence regularly makes you feel irritated, angry, belittled, anxious, depressed, or upset? Such people are toxic. Their effect on others is usually unintentional, but it's also unchangeable.

- Make a conscious effort to surround yourself with positive people. Seek them out, and when you find them, build a relationship. Move toward offloading your life of negative people. If there are toxic people in your life you can't totally detach from, work toward learning to set boundaries so they don't encroach on your well-being.

- When I suggest surrounding yourself with positivity, note that I don't mean people who are "relentlessly and obliviously happy." Positive people are not happy all the time. As you know, and as I've been emphasizing in this book, life is full of losses. When we experience loss, we grieve. We're naturally and necessarily sad. We might also be angry, numb, confused, anxious, and a bunch of other challenging emotions. I believe that positive people allow themselves to authentically experience life no matter what happens, all the while maintaining a sense of hope and awe as well as the intention to live and love fully.

- When you're around positive people, you're lifted up. You're buoyed by their spirit. You're taught how to love and grieve with authenticity and grace.

CARPE DIEM
Who's the most positive person in your life? Spend some time talking to or hanging out with this person today.

75.

REVIEW YOUR FINANCES

"Money isn't the most important thing in life,
but it's reasonably close to oxygen on the 'gotta have it' scale."
— Zig Ziglar

- Financial stressors can compound grief, and money troubles often make simmering family situations boil over.

- Have a meeting with your partner or an objective friend about your family finances. Gather up any necessary paperwork and go to neutral territory, like a coffee shop or restaurant. Talk openly about your financial situation and possible fixes.

- If you're in over your head financially, or if money talks get too emotional in your house, get help from someone objective. Ask a friend, or see a financial planner. Look for a non-commissioned professional certified by the National Association of Personal Financial Advisors or the Financial Planning Association.

- Don't risk your financial future over-caretaking for your adult children. Teach them self-responsibility. Some young adults may want to lay claim to their parents' net worth. Instead, encourage your children to build their own savings. I helped my children start Roth IRAs then turned the responsibility of growing the accounts over to them.

- If you're constantly worried about money, you won't be able to focus on your physical, cognitive, emotional, social, and spiritual well-being. Like grief anxiety, financial anxiety needs to be acknowledged and expressed. Putting a plan into place is also essential.

CARPE DIEM
What's the number one financial stress in your household?
Talk to your partner, a friend, or a financial consultant about it today.

76.

SPEND MORE TIME WITH YOUR OWN PARENTS

"We never know the love of a parent until we become parents ourselves."
— Henry Ward Beecher

- If your parents or in-laws are still alive, you're fortunate to still have the opportunity to spend time with them. While both of my parents have died, my wife's parents are still with us. We try to stay in contact and encourage our adult children to do the same.

- Now you know how you feel about your adult children and their separation from you. Your own parents felt and probably still feel similarly. They love you. They miss you. You're still and always will be their baby, even if you've got gray hair and a family of your own.

- I promise you that if you purposely and regularly make time to visit your parents from here forward, you will always be glad that you did. Actual visiting is best, but when you can't visit, call. Also send notes.

- If your relationship with your parents or in-laws is strained, now is the time to mend fences. Unless there are extenuating circumstances (such as a history of abuse), there's no excuse not to cherish the precious days you have left with your parents. After all, isn't it one of your deepest hopes that your own children will do the same some day?

CARPE DIEM
Put plans on the calendar to visit your own mom or dad.

77.

CONSIDER WHERE YOU WANT TO LIVE

"I felt like I had been looking for this place…my whole life."
— Their Eyes Were Watching God

- Size is a variable that can make the empty nest feel ridiculously empty. Are you or you and your partner living in a house that now seems way too big?

- If this rings true for you, both in terms of physical space and emotional response, it's time to reconsider. You don't need to do anything about it right away, but you do need to start the conversation with yourself or your partner. Always remember that if you're having an empty-nest-related thought or feeling, that's part of your grief, and your grief needs expression.

- When you're ready, start hitting open houses on weekends. Consider new possibilities—townhomes, apartments, patio homes, lofts, downtown, country, maybe even a different city altogether!

- Of course, there can be lots of advantages to staying put, so that might be your best fit. Remaining in the house in which you raised your family is not always about being practical. It can be about doing what you know in your heart is right for you. Our home is larger than my wife and I really need, but our adult children love to come home to it, and right now we still enjoy it. What about you?

- Grown children often experience grief when their parents start to talk about moving. Anticipate this, and respond with empathy.

CARPE DIEM
Ask yourself: if I could live anywhere, where would I live?

78.

SAY THANK YOU

---

*"We must find time to stop and thank the people
who make a difference in our lives."*
— John F. Kennedy

- Gratitude is a place of tenderness, empathy, love, and acceptance. Those are four qualities that we would all do well to foster.

- Start making a point of saying thank you—and meaning it. Thank your partner when she does something helpful or kind. Thank your friends. Thank your family members. Thank your coworkers. Thank your neighbors.

- Write one thank-you note, email, or text a day for the next month. Send them to all the people you've been meaning to thank but never have. Don't forget to thank your parents for loving you the best way they know how. Even if they've died, you may still consider writing them a letter of gratitude.

- Pay attention to how you feel after you write and send a note of thanks. You feel closer to the person you're thanking. You feel good about yourself. And you feel like you've sent some goodness and light into the world.

CARPE DIEM

Write a letter of thanks to your newly independent child. Tell him
all the things you're grateful for. Don't mention any of the hard or
challenging times in this particular note. Just include the good stuff.
I bet this will be a letter your child keeps forever.

79.

GET A KID FIX

"Time spent playing with children is never wasted."
— Dawn Lantero

- Sometimes I really miss my young children. I look at photos of my kids as babies, toddlers, and preschoolers and wish I could scoop them up again for a snuggle or a chase around the playground. Where did the time go?

- We already talked about the need to remember your children's childhoods as part of your mourning process. Memories are a treasure, even when they're tinged with the bittersweetness of what's past.

- I always loved watching my kids' faces light up (prior to their teen years) when I would arrive home from a trip. My youngest, Jaimie (now 21), would always wrap her arms around my legs and hold on as long as she could.

- If you're feeling baby lust, or little kid fever, try arranging a kid fix. Maybe you could offer to babysit a friend's children or volunteer at a school, a children's event, or your local Boys & Girls Club. A few hours with young children will not only feed your kid fix, it will probably help you realize that your own grown children are just the age they should be. As I write this, Sue and I are scheduled to play with two-year-old Sam this weekend. We are beyond excited for the opportunity, but I know we will need two or three days of rest after he leaves!

CARPE DIEM
Get a little kid fix today.

80.

ENJOY WHAT THE EARTH HAS TO OFFER

"The purpose of life is to live it, to taste experience to the utmost, to reach out eagerly and without fear for newer and richer experience."
— Eleanor Roosevelt

- As I get older and more and more people I have known and cared about die, I find myself wondering more about more about the possibilities of life after death. I'm not sure what it will be like, but I'm hopeful that it exists.

- Some people think that heaven will be just like earth, only better. Imagine the most beautiful lake you have ever seen, they say. Now multiply that by a hundred. That is what heaven is. Others describe a heaven that is completely unlike earth and beyond our imagining.

- In case the second group is right, I figure that we really ought to take advantage of what earth has to offer. I value spending time in nature, for example, so I make it a priority to go on hikes in the mountains, sight-seeing trips in the desert, and excursions to the beach.

- Which earthly delights make you swoon or fill you with wonder and delight? Being an empty-nester parent means you get to indulge yourself now. And maybe you'll find opportunities to share those loves with your adult child now and then.

CARPE DIEM
Spend at least half an hour in nature today.

81.

WORK THROUGH ESTRANGEMENT

"If you have never been hated by your child, you have never been a parent."
— Bette Davis

- Sometimes children take flight and sever ties. This is often, though not always, due to rocky relationships with family and/or extreme behavior (on either side) associated with drug abuse, legal troubles, or mental-health problems.

- If you're reading this book, you clearly would like to continue to have a relationship with your child. Know that estrangement can be worked through, though it may take time.

- Your child may need a period of defiance before he's ready to rebuild ties. This happens sometimes. It's not easy for you, and it can be dangerous for him. Set appropriate boundaries while letting the child know that you love him.

- Taking responsibility for any of your own behavior that may have contributed to the separation is also essential. Seeing a counselor is a good way to understand things afresh and step away from old, harmful patterns.

CARPE DIEM
Make an appointment with a counselor so you can get started
on developing the understanding and skills you need to rebuild
your relationship with your child.

82.

LET YOUR HAIR DOWN

"Do anything, but let it produce joy."
— Walt Whitman

- When we had children, we pretty much signed a contract that said, "I will try my best to always be responsible, dependable, and predictable." That's because our kids needed role models. They also deserved safety, routine, and emotional and financial security. So we fulfilled that contract, even though it was exhausting at times.

- But now? Now we can go hog wild! Now we can feel freer to experiment and even be a little irresponsible sometimes.

- Dessert for dinner? You bet. Drinking straight out of the milk carton? Why not? Leaving the dishes go for a day or two? Who cares? Singing in the shower then dancing naked around the house? What the heck!

- If you feel like being childish, be childish. Play! Splash in puddles and ride your bike without holding onto the handlebars. Reacquaint yourself with delight.

CARPE DIEM
Do something harmlessly irresponsible yet joyful today.

83.

THROW AN EMPTY-NEST PARTY

*"No one looks back on their life and remembers
the nights they got plenty of sleep."*
— Author Unknown

- You probably have friends who are going through the empty-nester years at the same time you are. Why not throw a party?

- Invite other parents whose children are in high school, college, or their twenties to join you for dinner or a potluck. If you explicitly make empty nesting the party's theme, the subject will naturally be discussed throughout the night. You'll hear other parents' challenges and perceived benefits, and your own thoughts and feelings will be affirmed. I'm not suggesting that the party have a maudlin support group atmosphere; I'm just saying that if you get a bunch of empty nesters together in a comfortable situation, they'll end up talking and listening to one another about their empty-nest thoughts, feelings, and experiences. That's mourning. That's what all of you need.

- Sometimes empty-nester grief can be the elephant in the room. Parents feel it inside, but they can be afraid to bring it up or make too much of it in conversation. That's because we as a culture are not very good at being open and honest about grief. An empty-nest party could help you and your friends feel more comfortable acknowledging and discussing it. People who need extra support will probably end up chatting with others who do as well. And who knows—maybe connections will blossom and acquaintances will grow into true friends.

CARPE DIEM
Put a party on the calendar. Get a friend to help you plan and prepare.

84.

BEWARE OF PRESSURE-COOKER SYNDROME

"Everyone has problems, and learning to share them is essential. Hiding pain requires an enormous amount of energy; sharing it is liberating."
— Carly Simon

- When a family experiences a significant loss of some kind, the household often experiences what I call "pressure-cooker syndrome." Everyone tends to have a high need to feel understood and a low capacity to understand others. In other words, each person is so naturally caught up in their own grief that they can't support anyone else, and they may even lash out at each other because everyone is feeling under-supported.

- Empty-nester couples are at risk for pressure-cooker syndrome. If you're bickering, treating each other passive-aggressively, or ignoring each other, it might be because you're projecting your feelings of grief onto your partner.

- If you still have children at home, they too can get caught up in this challenging situation.

- If your family is experiencing pressure-cooker syndrome, couples or family counseling can help you turn things around. It's not anything to be embarrassed about. On the contrary, seeking outside support is a sign of strength and commitment to the people you care most about in the whole world.

CARPE DIEM
If your household is pressure cooking,
find a healthy way to let off some steam together today.

85.

TAKE A DIGITAL RECKONING

*"The difference between technology and slavery is that slaves
are fully aware that they are not free."*
— Nassim Nicholas Taleb

- Those of us too old to be digital natives often bristle when everyone in the house is glued to their devices all the time. This was maddening with our teenagers, but it's downright disheartening when we ourselves perpetuate the habit.

- Keep an eye on digital overload in your life and relationships. If you and your partner are spending way more time online separately than you are on each other, together, then maybe it's time to have a conversation about ways to reconnect.

- Make a pact to enjoy technology with others. Pick a few different TV shows and commit to always watching them with friends. Listen to music as you prepare a meal or eat with people you care about. Try an audiobook on a road trip.

- Commit to spending at least one hour focused on nothing but another human being every day, with phones put away and all technology turned off. Talking and active listening are essential. You can combine conversation with an activity, if you want, such as playing a game or taking a walk together after dinner.

CARPE DIEM

Go on a digital cleanse. Whatever your most obsessive electronic habit is, forgo it for one day (taking care not to fill the time with other electronics) and see what new possibilities present themselves.

86.

ACT "AS IF"

"Begin to be now what you will be hereafter."
— William James

- Figuring out who you want to be now that your children are grown up is often a challenging task. Developing a new self takes mourning the old one as well as doing the hard work of excavating your divine spark.

- As you're working through the process, practice acting "as if." Acting "as if" is a technique that involves imagining you're already the something or someone you're thinking you might want to become. It's essentially a way to shortcut becoming.

- When you act "as if," you put on the manner and behavior of a person you are emulating. For example, if you decide that the new you will be a healthy weight (but the old you has weight to lose), you would act as if you were a thin person. You would make the choices of a thin person throughout the day, and whenever you found yourself falling into your old way of thinking, you would catch yourself and return to acting as if you were a thin person.

- This "fake-it-till-you-make-it" technique can also help you muster the courage to consider a new career or vocation. For instance, if you want to help poor children in your community but have no idea how to get started, act as if your participation really matters. You might get on the board of directors of a local nonprofit or apply for a job you're not fully qualified for yet but will be soon because you're acting "as if."

CARPE DIEM
What's something you would really like to do or be but don't know how?
Practice acting "as if" today.

87.

SEE THE WORLD ANEW

"I am not the same,
having seen the moon shine on the other side of the world."
— Mary Anne Radmacher

- When we're raising kids, we tend to spend most of our time in the same places. Children need routine, ritual, and a sense of safety. There are also financial and other practical constraints. So we limit our travel. We're at home a lot. We're tethered to our communities. Often, we even take family vacations in the same familiar spots.

- But now, finally, we're free to travel. We can pick up and go whenever the mood strikes—alone, with our partner, or with friends. We'll be leaving our empty nest behind, but we'll be bringing our grief with us. And our grief, as seen from the new vantage points, will shift and change. This momentum is good.

- Visiting new places also stimulates our brains. It opens us to new thoughts and feelings. Travel also helps us work on our evolving self-identities, as it gives us a richer understanding of our own personal context in the world.

- All of these benefits of travel are available on a modest budget, by the way. We can go backpacking, sleep in senior adult hostels, take car trips, and visit friends in other cities.

CARPE DIEM
Make plans to go somewhere this week that you've never been before,
even if it's in your own community.

88.

RECAPTURE YOUR LISTENING SKILLS

"One of the most sincere forms of respect is actually listening to what another has to say."
— Bryant H. McGill

- As busy parents, many of us have forgotten how to be good, active listeners. It's no wonder…we've been running around like chickens with our heads cut off for a good twenty-plus years. There was always so much that needed doing!

- What a gift it is to be able to dwell in the present moment again. Part of this gift is what happens when we actively listen to another human being—our child, our partner, our family member, our friend. If we recapture the art of listening, we can often recapture trust, tenderness, and intimacy. We create the conditions for love to blossom again.

- Active listening means being totally present to another human being. It means turning off and away from all distractions and attending fully to the other person. It involves listening without judging or prematurely offering solutions. It includes offering empathy and unconditional love.

- Parenting an adult child is about presence and active listening. It is no longer about chastising, admonishing, dictating, or playing judge. Only when guidance is asked for do we offer it. This is a challenging facet of the empty-nest transition, but the sooner we begin to work toward it, the sooner we find ourselves strengthening our new relationship. Developmentally, our young adult children have needed to push away as they launch into the world. Our active listening can invite them to come back after this necessary going away.

CARPE DIEM
Commit to fully, actively listening to someone you care about
for a full ten minutes today.

89.

ADOPT A PET

"Whatever else happened, she wanted a dog in her life."
— Jonathan Franzen

- Companion animals add a lot of joy to our lives. Yes, they also take effort and money—but not that much compared to kids!

- I've always had dogs, and I can't imagine my life without them. As my children began leaving home, I often turned to my dogs for comfort and companionship. Zoey and Laney are my buddies.

- At any given time, there are millions of at-risk dogs, cats, bunnies, birds, and other animals at shelters waiting to be adopted. If you're not ready to adopt, you can foster pets instead. Shelters always need volunteers to take animals to their homes and give them lots of love and attention while they're waiting for their forever homes.

- Of course a pet can never replace a child, but a pet can add simple love and affection to your days—assets you need right now. And pretty soon you'll never know how you ever got along without him.

CARPE DIEM

Today, look into adopting or fostering a pet. Fostering is a wonderful way to add a little spark to your life without the full-blown commitment of a forever pet.

90.

TAKE A GAP YEAR

*"In wisdom gathered over time I have found
that every experience is a form of exploration."*
— Ansel Adams

- You know how kids sometimes take a gap year between high school and college to mature a little and also make time for exploration, such as travel or volunteerism? Well, we parents can take a gap year too!

- A gap year is a transition year. That first empty-nester year is one of the biggest transition years in life.

- Choose a 12-month window to explore your changing self. You don't have to meet a particular, stated set of goals if you don't want to. Instead, think of it as time you're setting aside to figure things out. Ask yourself: where do I go from here?

- Taking a year off from your career would be a special luxury. But even if you can't (or don't want to) do that, you can still explore in your free time. Travel, take a class, look into a new job, start a side business, or try a smorgasbord of new hobbies. Journal about all your new experiences so you'll have a record to look back on after the year is over.

CARPE DIEM
Have a brainstorming chat with your partner or a close friend
about the idea of an empty-nester gap year.

91.

SAVOR THE FLAVOR OF DINING WITHOUT KIDS

"As a child my family's menu consisted of two choices: take it, or leave it."
— Buddy Hackett

- Daily cooking for a family is a lot different than cooking for just one or two. Depending on what your family's eating habits have been lately, the new grocery shopping/cooking/leftovers routine will likely take some experimenting and getting used to.

- Now might be the time to add different foods to your menu. What do you love but never prepared because the kids didn't like it? What have you always wanted to try? What's something you enjoy but rarely bought because it was too expensive in family-sized portions?

- Dining together is a sensual bonding ritual for couples. Try some new recipes and restaurants. Many places have excellent happy hour deals. Savor eating more slowly and learning to have grown-up dinner conversation again.

CARPE DIEM
Stop by your favorite special-occasion grocer or deli today,
and pick up several unusual delicacies.

92.

DATE YOUR PARTNER

"Staying in love is the hard part."
— Emily Lingenfelser

- Especially if you and your partner have been together for a long time, you probably got into at least somewhat of a rut during the child-rearing years. It's practically impossible to take great care of your relationship at the same time you're taking great care of kids.

- If you haven't already, it's time to start refocusing on your relationship to your partner not as a co-parent but as a companion, confidant, and lover.

- The time-honored, effective, fun way to do it? Dating!

- Once a week, go on a date. It doesn't need to be fancy or expensive, but it does need to be just the two of you, doing something special together, focused on communicating and having a good time.

- Trying new things together will help you re-bond. Instead of a movie or dinner at your usual hangout, think mini-golf. Or a cooking class. Or a museum, scenic drive, or coffee, beer, or wine tasting.

CARPE DIEM
Plan a date with your life partner for sometime this week.

93.

MOVE PLANS TO THE FRONT BURNER

"Twenty years from now you will be more disappointed by the things that you didn't do than by the ones you did do, so throw off the bowlines, sail away from the safe harbor, catch the trade winds in your sails. Explore, dream, discover."

— H. Jackson Brown

- Parents are often forced to put long-cherished wishes, dreams, and goals on the back burner. After all, the family's and children's needs have always come before the individual parent's or the couple's wants.

- What's been on your back burner for years and maybe even decades? It's time to slide a few of those dreams to the front burner.

- Start by making a list of all your back-burnered goals and activities. A jumping-off point can be this prompt: I've always wanted to... Write until you run out of ideas.

- Now divide your list into three categories: Easy, Moderate, and Challenging. Easy wishes are those you can accomplish in a few hours, such as dying your hair or getting a massage. Moderate wishes take a bigger commitment of time, energy, and maybe money: painting your bedroom, taking a weekend trip, signing up for a cooking class. Challenging wishes are the biggies: training for and completing a half-marathon, taking an international vacation, learning a foreign language, changing your career.

- Finally, pick one item from each category and get started.

CARPE DIEM
Do the list-making activity described above.

94.

GROW YOURSELF

"It's not only children who grow. Parents do too. As much as we watch to see what our children do with their lives, they are watching us to see what we do with ours. I can't tell my children to reach for the sun. All I can do is reach for it myself."

— Joyce Maynard

- You've finally gotten your kids through school. Maybe it's time to enroll yourself.

- People with a growth mindset understand that they have the power to enhance their abilities through continued learning and hard work. In other words, brains and talent are just a starting point. After that, it's up to you.

- Cultivating a growth mindset matters because studies show that it makes people both happier and more successful at whatever their chosen endeavors are.

- So, take classes. Learn new things. Meet new people. Practice the skills you want to improve.

- Turns out that you *can* teach an old dog new tricks—as long as the old dog is willing to try.

CARPE DIEM
Take one small step to grow yourself today.

95.

GET READY TO CATCH THE BOOMERANG

---

*"Anticipating a boomerang child seems the odds-on thing to do.
Think about furnishing—hello, sleeper sofa!—with this in mind."*
— Jean Chatzky

- Empty nesting is particularly challenging these days because not only is this generation of young adults taking flight later and in fits and starts, they're also returning home in record numbers. About 32 percent of 18 to 24-year-old Americans live with their parents—more than at any other time since World War II.

- Talk proactively with your partner or a friend about setting house rules for adult children living at home. While you may want to be flexible, adopting a "wait and see" approach, you will probably find it helpful to have at least discussed the issue before it arises.

- Under what circumstances are adult children allowed to return to live in your home? When they do, will they be asked to pay rent or other expenses? Who will do the cooking, cleaning, laundry, etc.? What about drug/alcohol use, overnight guests, curfew, etc.?

- Living with adult children was common before WWII, and I'm not suggesting it's wrong. In fact, multigenerational living can be richly rewarding. I am suggesting, though, that it's good to think about before your child pulls up in your driveway with all his belongings crammed into his car and says, "I'm back!"

- If this has already happened for you, how is it going? Do you need to set boundaries or timelines?

CARPE DIEM
Talk with someone about the possibility of the boomerang
phenomenon hitting your home.

96.

IMAGINE YOURSELF AT 96

*"It's better to look back on life and say,
'I can't believe I did that' than, 'I wish I did that.'"*
— Author Unknown

- Project yourself forward in time. Imagine you're 80. What are you doing? What are you no longer doing?

- Now imagine your 96-year-old self looking back on your life. What does your older self wish you had done differently?

- What are you most proud of? What do you wish you had spent more time doing? What do you wish you had spent less time doing? What are your biggest regrets?

- The great thing about this exercise is that while you can't change the actual past, you can change the portion of the imagined past that is your current self's present and future. You still have time.

CARPE DIEM

Write your own best-case-scenario obituary. What does it mention that you haven't yet done, accomplished, or prioritized? Get started on those things today.

97.

SAY THE UNSAID

"When you give yourself permission to communicate what matters to you in every situation, you will have peace despite rejection or disapproval. Putting a voice to your soul helps you to let go of the negative energy of fear and regret."

— Shannon L. Alder

- If you knew you would die tomorrow, what would you say to the people you care about today?

- Say it. Say it now.

- Call your child and say whatever is on your heart. If calling won't work, write a letter or send an email or text.

- Start with, "I just wanted to let you know that…" Say whatever matters most. Say whatever you would fell terrible about having left unsaid if you never got the chance to say it.

CARPE DIEM
Call, text, or write someone who's important to you today.
Start with: "I just wanted to let you know that…"

98.

CELEBRATE YOUR PARENTING SUCCESS

*"The more you praise and celebrate your life,
the more there is in life to celebrate."*
— Oprah Winfrey

- Raising children all the way through to independence is a feat of epic proportions.

- Parenting is a 24/7, 365 job. You've been on duty for years and years solid. Not only that, but if you're like most parents I know, you gave it your all. You weren't perfect, but you were perfectly committed.

- Just think…how many kisses and hugs did you give? How many lunches did you pack? How many loads of laundry? How many car rides? How many activities did you attend? How many gifts and meals and words of encouragement?

- You deserve congratulations and thanks. Your children probably aren't mature enough yet to thank you, so you'll have to thank yourself. A special empty-nester vacation is in order, or if budgets are tight, a special staycation. Treat yourself for a whole week solid. Lavish yourself with your special-occasion activities, foods, and pampering.

CARPE DIEM
Plan a special empty-nester vacation or staycation for sometime soon.

99.

KNOW THAT PARENTING NEVER ENDS

"Be nice to your children, for they will choose your rest home."
— Phyllis Diller

- No matter what, you will always be your child's parent. It sounds obvious, but it's important that we remind ourselves of this as the details of our relationships with our children change.

- As our children continue to mature, perhaps even having their own children one day, they will grow to understand our role as parents more deeply. If we are lucky, we will be rewarded with the joy of getting to be grandparents!

- The cycle of life will continue, yet we will still be parents. Even if and when we are grandparents, we will still be parents.

- The twenty or so years that we parented our children most intensely was one phase in lives. We experienced our own childhoods before that, and now we are embarking on a third phase. It can be a good one. It can be a rich one. Let's mourn our way through the transition and find out.

CARPE DIEM
Plant a tree in your child's honor, even if you don't tell her she's the reason.

100.

PLACE A PHOTO WHERE YOU'LL SEE IT OFTEN

"A hundred years from now it will not matter what my bank account was, the sort of house I lived in, or the kind of car I drove, but the world may be different because I was important in the life of a child."
— Forest Witcraft

- Pick one of your favorite photos of your children when they were little and place a copy of it where you'll see it often—on your dresser, as the wallpaper image on your computer, in your TV room.

- The tenderness you feel and the tears that spring to your eyes whenever you see that photo are signs that the history of your love for your children and your gratitude over having had the privilege to be a parent are still very much alive. Your grief lives in that moment, but so does your love.

- Your hopeful love lives in the next photo you will take of your child, and the next and the next.

- We give ourselves to our children, and then, because we have raised them to be strong, independent individuals with hopes and dreams of their own, they leave us. They take a part of us with them. This is both a painful and a miraculous privilege.

CARPE DIEM
Place a photo of your child where you will see it often.
Give it a kiss every day

A FINAL WORD

"There's no such thing as a perfect parent. So just be a real one."
— Sue Atkins

This parenting thing sure is hard. As with all life's greatest challenges, we couldn't understand just how hard until we experienced it for ourselves. Of course, we also couldn't appreciate the abiding love and profound joys of raising children until we experienced them, either.

So here we are. I hope you've found a measure of affirmation and support in this little book. Remember that our empty-nester grief is not only real, it is normal and necessary. And it can be painful and long-lasting. But if you learn to embrace your grief and express it openly and fully each day, over time it will begin to soften. You will eventually transcend the transition of your children leaving home and integrate the loss into your continued life.

Speaking of your continued life, in the Introduction I also promised that this book would help you rediscover your own divine spark. It's true, but you've got to work at it. Faithfully applying yourself to the Ideas focused on nurturing your inner truths, passions, and relationships will indeed help you reach for the sun.

I once heard there are seven things every child needs to hear:

1. I love you.

2. I'm proud of you.

3. I'm sorry.

4. I forgive you.

5. I'm listening.

6. This is your responsibility.

7. You've got what it takes.

Let's continue to speak these words to our adult children. We love them so much, and we want more than anything for them to be happy, healthy, and secure. As we transition from adult-to-child to adult-to-adult relationships with our sons and daughters, let's remember that we're responsible *to* them, but we're no longer responsible *for* them.

And while we're at it, let's speak those same seven phrases to ourselves. We're worthy, if weathered, individuals. We've earned this time for ourselves. We've got what it takes to live and love fully the rest of our precious days here on earth.

ALSO BY ALAN WOLFELT

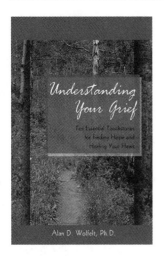

Understanding Your Grief
Ten Essential Touchstones for Finding Hope and Healing Your Heart

One of North America's leading grief educators, Dr. Alan Wolfelt has written many books about healing in grief. This book is his most comprehensive, covering the essential lessons that mourners have taught him in his three decades of working with the bereaved.

In compassionate, down-to-earth language, *Understanding Your Grief* describes ten touchstones—or trail markers—that are essential physical, emotional, cognitive, social, and spiritual signs for mourners to look for on their journey through grief.

Think of your grief as a wilderness—a vast, inhospitable forest. You must journey through this wilderness. To find your way out, you must become acquainted with its terrain and learn to follow the sometimes hard-to-find trail that leads to healing. In the wilderness of your grief, the touchstones are your trail markers. They are the signs that let you know you are on the right path. When you learn to identify and rely on the touchstones, you will find your way to hope and healing.

ISBN 978-1-879651-35-7 • 176 pages
softcover • $14.95

The Ten Essential Touchstones:

1. Open to the presence of your loss.
2. Dispel misconceptions about grief.
3. Embrace the uniqueness of your grief.
4. Explore your feelings of loss.
5. Recognize you are not crazy.
6. Understand the six needs of mourning.
7. Nurture yourself.
8. Reach out for help.
9. Seek reconciliation, not resolution.
10. Appreciate your transformation.

Companion
PRESS

All Dr. Wolfelt's publications can be ordered by mail from:
Companion Press
3735 Broken Bow Road
Fort Collins, CO 80526
(970) 226-6050
www.centerforloss.com

ALSO BY ALAN WOLFELT

Grief One Day at a Time
365 Meditations to Help You Heal After Loss

After a loved one dies, each day can be a struggle. But each day, you can also find comfort and understanding in this daily companion. With one brief entry for every day of the calendar year, this little book by beloved grief counselor Dr. Alan Wolfelt offers small, one-day-at-a-time doses of guidance and healing.

ISBN 978-1-61722-238- 2 • 384 pages • softcover • $14.95

"This is a fabulous little meditation for those who are grieving. Our bereavement teams at Sangre de Cristo Hospice utilize this in our bereavement groups."
— Amazon reviewer

"The best daily reader on grief that I have found."
— Amazon reviewer

"I love this book so much! I recently lost my father to a brutal disease, too early in his senior life. This book has been so helpful for me. Having this book to turn to on a daily basis is helping me cope. I would be a lot more lost without this book."
— Amazon reviewer

"Very nice book with short, less than five-minute daily meditations for anyone who is suffering the loss of a loved one. Highly recommend!"
— Amazon reviewer

Companion
PRESS

All Dr. Wolfelt's publications can be ordered by mail from:
Companion Press
3735 Broken Bow Road
Fort Collins, CO 80526
(970) 226-6050
www.centerforloss.com

ALSO BY ALAN WOLFELT

Healing the Adult Child's Grieving Heart
100 Practical Ideas

Offering heartfelt and simple advice, this book provides realistic suggestions and relief for an adult child whose parent has died. Practical advice is presented in a one-topic-per-page format that does not overwhelm but instead provides small, immediate ways for the reader to understand and embrace their grief.

ISBN 978-1-879651-31-9 • 128 pages
softcover • $11.95

"I bought this book shortly after my father passed away, and thought it was so good I ordered more copies for my siblings. This book is divided into subjects with text limited to one page per topic. While normally I like more detail, the author knows that in times of grief the brain more readily accepts smaller bits of information. I usually read one or two pages at a time. I also think this book would be very helpful to anyone regardless of religious beliefs."

— Amazon reviewer

"This is a must for anyone who has lost a parent. My book is marked, bent, and goes with me everywhere. I am new to grieving, and I find this a helpful guide toward healing."

— Amazon reviewer

"Simple, relevant, and gentle. I ordered one for my brother and sister to ease us into dialogue. Thank you, Dr. Wolfelt."

— Anne Chapman

Companion
P R E S S

All Dr. Wolfelt's publications can be ordered by mail from:
Companion Press
3735 Broken Bow Road
Fort Collins, CO 80526
(970) 226-6050
www.centerforloss.com

ALSO BY ALAN WOLFELT

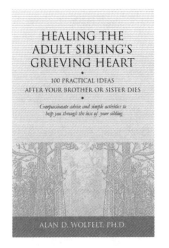

Healing the Adult Sibling's Grieving Heart
100 Practical Ideas After Your Brother or Sister Dies

Compassionate and heartfelt, this collection offers 100 practical ideas to help you understand and mourn the death of a sibling. The principles of grief and mourning are clearly defined, accompanied by action-oriented tips for embracing grief.

Whether a sibling has died as a young or older adult, whether the death was sudden or anticipated, this resource offers compassionate guidance for the normal and necessary journey through grief.

978-1-879651-29-6 • 128 pages • softcover • $11.95

"I was so grateful there was a book out there to help me in my grief when my brother died unexpectedly. The book let me know that it was OK to be sad, cry, and most of all to be easy on myself."
— Barbara Franklin

"At a time when I am hurting tremendously following the sudden, tragic death of my brother, this book has been a really wonderful source of validation and support. I like the fact that it's a very simple read, and that I can pick it up now and then and get a few helpful thoughts without spending a lot of time and energy. I even bought copies for my two sisters and sent them as gifts."
— Amazon reviewer

Companion
PRESS

All Dr. Wolfelt's publications can be ordered by mail from:
Companion Press
3735 Broken Bow Road
Fort Collins, CO 80526
(970) 226-6050
www.centerforloss.com

ALSO BY ALAN WOLFELT

Healing Your Grief About Aging
100 Practical Ideas on Growing Older with Confidence, Meaning, and Grace

by Alan D. Wolfelt, Ph.D. and Kirby J. Duvall, M.D.

Getting older goes hand in hand with losses of many kinds—ending careers, empty nests, illness, the death of loved ones—and this book by one of the world's most beloved grief counselors helps readers acknowledge and mourn the many losses of aging while also offering advice for living better in older age.

The 100 practical tips and activities address the emotional, spiritual, cognitive, social, and physical needs of seniors who want to age authentically and gracefully. Whether you've just entered your 50s or are well on your way to the century mark, this book promises elder-friendly tips for comfort, laughter, and inspiration.

ISBN 978-1-61722-171-2 • 128 pages • softcover • $11.95

"This is a very easy read that can be helpful at different times of life. Alan Wolfelt has such a gift for teaching people how to look for the joy in life and guide them on the inevitable journey toward death."
— Amazon reviewer

Companion
PRESS

All Dr. Wolfelt's publications can be ordered by mail from:
Companion Press
3735 Broken Bow Road
Fort Collins, CO 80526
(970) 226-6050
www.centerforloss.com

ALSO BY ALAN WOLFELT

The Depression of Grief
Coping with Your Sadness and Knowing When to Get Help

When someone you love dies, it's normal and necessary to grieve. Grief is the thoughts and feelings you have inside you, and sadness is often the most prominent and painful emotion. In other words, it's normal to be depressed after a loss. This compassionate guide will help you understand your natural depression, express it in ways that will help you heal, and know when you may be experiencing a more severe or clinical depression that would be eased by professional treatment. A section for caregivers that explores the new DSM-5 criteria for Major Depression is also included.

ISBN 978-1-61722-193-4 • 128 pages • softcover • $14.95

"This enlightening book revealed to me that I am not flawed, and it further gave me the strength to go back and do a bit more work so I could truly mourn the loss of my mom and start living life once again."

— Kerry Bratton

Companion
PRESS

All Dr. Wolfelt's publications can be ordered by mail from:
Companion Press
3735 Broken Bow Road
Fort Collins, CO 80526
(970) 226-6050
www.centerforloss.com

ALSO BY ALAN WOLFELT

When Your Pet Dies
A Guide to Mourning, Remembering, and Healing

Affirming that profound grief is often normal and necessary after the death of a beloved pet, this book helps mourners understand why their feelings are so strong and helps them embrace and express their grief. Included are practical suggestions for mourning as well as remembering and memorializing your pet.

Interspersed with real-life stories of pet owners, the chapters cover what makes the grief following pet loss unique, common thoughts and feelings, pet funerals and burial or cremation, celebrating the life of your pet, coping with feelings about euthanasia, helping children understand the death of a pet, things to keep in mind before getting another pet, and more.

ISBN 978-1-879651-36-4 • 80 pages • softcover • $9.95

"This book definitely helped me as I grieved the loss of my precious little girl. It was nice to read and know that all the sadness and various other emotions and thoughts were not just mine; many like myself had gone through this, and it was normal. Very short and well thought out. The stories of other people and their precious furry friends are heartwarming."
— Amazon reviewer

"So well written and just what I needed. I recommend to any pet lover."
— Heather Gilbert

Companion
PRESS

All Dr. Wolfelt's publications can be ordered by mail from:
Companion Press
3735 Broken Bow Road
Fort Collins, CO 80526
(970) 226-6050
www.centerforloss.com

TRAINING AND SPEAKING ENGAGEMENTS

To contact Dr. Wolfelt about speaking engagements or training opportunities at his Center for Loss and Life Transition, email him at DrWolfelt@centerforloss.com